TEXT AND PERFORMANCE

General Editor: Michael Scott

The series is designed to introduce sixth-form and undergraduate students to the themes, continuing vitality and performance of major dramatic works. The attention given to production aspects is an element of special importance, responding to the invigoration given to literary study by the work of leading contemporary critics.

The prime aim is to present each play as a vital experience in the mind of the reader – achieved by analysis of the text in relation to its themes and theatricality. Emphasis is accordingly placed on the relevance of the work to the modern reader and the world of today. At the same time, traditional views are presented and appraised, forming the basis from which a creative response to the text can develop.

In each volume, Part One: *Text* discusses certain key themes or problems, the reader being encouraged to gain a stronger perception both of the inherent character of the work and also of variations in interpreting it. Part Two: *Performance* examines the ways in which these themes or problems have been handled in modern productions, and the approaches and techniques employed to enhance the play's accessibility to modern audiences.

A synopsis of the play is given and an outline of its major sources, and a concluding Reading List offers guidance to the student's independent study of the work.

THE
WINTER'S TALE

Text and Performance

R. P. DRAPER

MACMILLAN

First published 1985

Published by
Higher and Further Education Division
MACMILLAN PUBLISHERS LTD
Houndmills, Basingstoke, Hampshire RG21 2XS
and London
Companies and representatives
throughout the world

Typeset by
Wessex Typesetters
Frome, Somerset

Printed in Hong Kong

British Library Cataloguing in Publication Data
Shakespeare, William
The winter's tale. – (Text and performance)
1. Shakespeare, William. Winter's tale
I. Title   II. Draper, R. P.   III. Series
822.3′3   PR2839
ISBN 0–333–34981–4

CONTENTS

Illustrations will be found in Part Two

6

ACKNOWLEDGEMENTS

Quotations of the text of the play are from the New Penguin Shakespeare edition (1969), edited by Ernest Schanzer.

Source details for the illustrations are given with the relevant captions to the photographs.

I should like to take this opportunity of thanking the staff of the Nuffield Library at the Shakespeare Centre, Stratford-upon-Avon, and of the National Sound Archive, London, for their helpfulness in making materials available to me. My debt to a wide variety of Shakespeare scholars and dramatic critics will be apparent to the reader from the attributions given in the text; but I should particularly like to thank Professor J. R. Mulryne for drawing my attention to MA theses by two of his students, Christine Wallwork and Kathleen Gledhill, which deal with aspects of the RSC productions discussed in Part Two of this book.

GENERAL EDITOR'S PREFACE

For many years a mutual suspicion existed between the theatre director and the literary critic of drama. Although in the first half of the century there were important exceptions, such was the rule. A radical change of attitude, however, has taken place over the last thirty years. Critics and directors now increasingly recognise the significance of each other's work and acknowledge their growing awareness of interdependence. Both interpret the same text, but do so according to their different situations and functions. Without the director, the designer and the actor, a play's existence is only partial. They revitalise the text with action, enabling the drama to live fully at each performance. The academic critic investigates the script to elucidate its textual problems, understand its conventions and discover how it operates. He may also propose his view of the work, expounding what he considers to be its significance.

Dramatic texts belong therefore to theatre and to literature. The aim of the 'Text and Performance' series is to achieve a fuller recognition of how both enhance our enjoyment of the play. Each volume follows the same basic pattern. Part One provides a critical introduction to the play under discussion, using the techniques and criteria of the literary critic in examining the manner in which the work operates through language, imagery and action. Part Two takes the enquiry further into the play's theatricality by focusing on selected productions of recent times so as to illustrate points of contrast and comparison in the interpretation of different directors and actors, and to demonstrate how the drama has worked on the modern stage. In this way the series seeks to provide a lively and informative introduction to major plays in their text and performance.

MICHAEL SCOTT

PLOT SYNOPSIS AND SOURCE

After a nine months' stay with his friend Leontes, King of Sicilia, Polixenes, King of Bohemia, wishes to return home. Leontes urges him to remain, and, on being refused, asks his wife, Hermione, to help. She succeeds, but he jealously suspects her of having committed adultery with Polixenes. He orders his counsellor, Camillo, to poison Polixenes. Camillo, however, reveals all, and flees from Sicilia with Polixenes. Leontes separates Hermione from her son, Mamillius, and has her imprisoned, though he also sends to the Oracle at Delphos for confirmation of her guilt. A baby girl is born to Hermione, and one of her ladies, Paulina, brings it to Leontes. Leontes orders Antigonus (Paulina's husband) to expose it in some wilderness outside Sicilia. At her trial Hermione bravely defends herself and submits to the Oracle, which pronounces her innocent, adding that 'the King shall live without an heir, if that which is lost be not found'. Mamillius dies, and Hermione also appears to die; whereupon Leontes acknowledges his injustice and repents. The baby is abandoned on the sea-coast of Bohemia, and those who brought it there, including Antigonus, are killed. The child, however, is rescued by an old shepherd. Sixteen years elapse, and the child, now grown into the shepherdess, Perdita, presides at a sheep-shearing festival, at which her lover, Florizel, son of Polixenes, is present in the guise of a shepherd, as are his father and Camillo, also in disguise. When Florizel states his intention to marry Perdita, Polixenes breaks off the match with terrible threats. Camillo advises Florizel to take Perdita to Sicilia and present himself as an ambassador from Polixenes. An exchange of clothes is arranged between Florizel and Autolycus (a rogue introduced at the sheep-shearing); and Autolycus makes the old shepherd believe that he can persuade Polixenes to show mercy to him and his son. In Sicilia Leontes is urged by his courtiers to remarry, but Paulina reminds him of the oracle. Florizel and Perdita arrive, and, when Polixenes follows in hot pursuit, Leontes agrees to intercede on their behalf. Thanks to the old shepherd, Perdita's true identity is revealed, the two kings are reconciled, and Perdita is united with her father. Finally, Paulina brings them all to view a statue of Hermione, which astonishingly comes to life; the Queen is restored to her husband and daughter, and Leontes joins Paulina and Camillo in wedlock.

SOURCE

The main source is Robert Greene's *Pandosto* (1588). Greene's story is altered in certain respects, and new characters are added, including Paulina, Antigonus and Autolycus. Shakespeare also adds Antigonus's being torn to pieces by a bear and the sheep-shearing festival. (See *Narrative and Dramatic Sources of Shakespeare*, ed. Geoffrey Bullough, vol. VIII.)

PART ONE: TEXT

1 INTRODUCTION

For some time now it has been recognised that the four plays
(excluding *Henry VIII*) which Shakespeare wrote towards the
end of his career as a dramatist – *Pericles* (1607–8), *Cymbeline*
(1609–10), *The Winter's Tale* (1611) and *The Tempest* (1611) form
a relatively homogeneous group. In each of them Shakespeare
shows a strong interest in the relations between parents and
children and makes use of plots which involve loss and finding
again, division and reconciliation, destruction and renewal.
For this reason they might be regarded as tragi-comedies,
though the term has associations with the artificially strained
sensationalism of Beaumont and Fletcher which are inappropriate to the organic nature of Shakespeare's combining
of tragedy and comedy, above all in *The Winter's Tale*. As an
experienced man of the theatre, and one who strove to please
his audience 'every day' [*Twelfth Night*, v i 394], it is reasonable
to suppose that he might have been responding to a taste for
dramatic piquancy that seems to have characterised a sophisticated section of the early-seventeenth-century theatre public,
and this may well have chimed in with the opportunities offered
the King's Men (the company for which Shakespeare was
resident playwright) by their recent acquisition of an indoor
theatre at Blackfriars. But, if this did have an influence on the
form of the late plays, they were certainly intended for
performance at the open-air Globe as well, and this theatre still
drew the largest, though not necessarily the most commercially
profitable, audiences. *The Winter's Tale* may have been performed first at the Blackfriars Theatre, but it was soon put on at
the old theatre, as we know from Simon Forman's *Booke of Plaies*,
which records a performance 'at the glob 1611 the 15 of Maye'
(Variorum edn, p. 318).

The emphasis on dancing and music which is notable in
these plays may also have something to do with conditions at

Blackfriars, and may reflect the current vogue in Court circles for the more static and scenically splendid form of the masque. The masque may likewise have encouraged the greater use of allegory and symbolism and effects of the 'marvellous', such as Jupiter's descent '*in thunder and lightning, sitting upon an eagle*' in *Cymbeline*, v iv, and the statue's coming to life in *The Winter's Tale*, v iii. But Shakespeare might equally well be seen as harking back to the past rather than reacting to the latest fashion. Much of the atmosphere of these plays, including the creation of deliberately archaic linguistic effects, belongs, like the stories from which he takes his plots, to the world of romance with its idealised lovers and astonishing adventures. The immediate source of *The Winter's Tale* is Greene's prose romance *Pandosto* (first published in 1588), and the kind of story that *Pandosto* represents has a long history going as far back as the Greek romances of the second century AD, of which Longus's *Daphnis and Chloe* is the best-known example.

The title of *The Winter's Tale* would suggest that Shakespeare is in some sense returning to a more primitive type of drama here, though, paradoxically, it is also one of the most original and experimental of his plays. The mention of 'tale' is echoed at various points within the text, as when, for example, Hermione invites Mamillius to entertain her with a merry tale and Mamillius replies with

> A sad tale's best for winter. I have one
> Of sprites and goblins.   [ii i 25–6]

Similarly, one of the gentlemen who in v ii are discussing the reunion of Perdita and Leontes exclaims, 'This news, which is called true, is so like an old tale that the verity of it is in strong suspicion' [27–9]; and when he asks what became of Antigonus another replies, 'Like an old tale still, which will have matter to rehearse, though credit be asleep and not an ear open: he was torn to pieces with a bear' [59–61]. The latter reference in particular glances back at a piece of the play's action (the death of Antigonus in iii iii) which some critics have found amateurish in stagecraft, others deliberately grotesque. Nevill Coghill is nearer the truth when he pronounces it 'a dazzling piece of *avant-garde* work', a means by which tragedy is transformed into comedy (*Shakespeare Survey 11*, p. 35). It is the dramatic equivalent of the narrative distancing effected by the archaic manner of 'an old tale'. Shakespeare himself seems aware of the different reactions it might provoke and seems to want to forestall criticism. What such a scene, and the whole play, demands is a readiness to put aside niggling rationality; which, however, is not to say that *The Winter's Tale* is pure fairy tale, nor even that the audience's realistic expectations must somehow be drugged into inactivity. A flexible response is required – a condition of mind in which the audience can be aware of different, and even contradictory, levels of meaning, just as a child can respond to a story by seeming to immerse himself completely in its imaginative world and yet remain easily aware that it is only a story.

The statue scene is again one in which Shakespeare seems to show awareness of the possibility of a sceptical response, and yet builds his reckoning of it into the text in such a way that it can be interpreted as either an attempt to lift the audience on to a level of supra-rational understanding – 'It is required / You do awake your faith' [v iii 94–5] – or a tacit recognition of the inevitable fragility of the illusion that is being created, shared and conspiratorially enjoyed with the audience – 'What fine chisel / Could ever yet cut breath?' [v iii 78–9]. Either way, as many reviewers have observed, the scene always works very well in the actual theatre, and it is equally effective with the most naïve and the most sophisticated of audiences. That it does so is a tribute to Shakespeare's dramatic craftsmanship and his highly developed sense of theatrical convention, which enables him to work the magic of illusion with seemingly passionate conviction, while yet retaining consciousness of it as a deliberately contrived stage effect.

2   STRUCTURE

The objections once made to the violation in *The Winter's Tale* of the so-called 'unities' of time and place, and in particular the leaving of a gap of sixteen years between Acts III and IV, no longer disturb critics, and never much bothered living audiences of the play. As Dr Johnson observed, 'Time is, of all modes of existence, most obsequious to the imagination; a lapse of years is as easily conceived as a passage of hours' (*Preface to Shakespeare*, 1765). When he so wished, Shakespeare could write a play perfectly in accord with the classical rules, as he showed at the beginning of his career in *The Comedy of Errors* and again at the end (immediately after *The Winter's Tale*) in *The Tempest*. If disregard for these rules appears more marked in *The Winter's Tale* than in any other of his plays, it is not because Shakespeare treated the question of time as insignificant, but precisely because he wished to give it exceptional dramatic prominence.

Inga-Stina Ewbank ('The Triumph of Time in *The Winter's Tale*', *Review of English Literature*, 1964) has shown how time-consciousness permeates the play, creating a serious theme out of 'The Triumph of Time', which is the sub-title of *Pandosto*, but which in Greene means no more than that the misadventures which Fortune introduces into the lives of the characters are at last partially overcome by the equally adventitious working of Fortune. Shakespeare, by contrast, offers a perspective in which the present is seen in relation to the past and the future. For example, the play opens with a dialogue between Camillo and Archidamus which refers to the present friendship between Polixenes and Leontes, but also glances back to their childhood association [I i 22–4], in a way that is picked up and elaborated by Polixenes in the following scene [I ii 67–71], and looks forward to the future made seemingly bright in the person of Leontes' young son, Mamillius [I i 33–9]. The dashing of that promise by Leontes' outrageous jealousy is emphasised by the pronouncement of the Oracle that '*the King shall live without an heir, if that which is lost be not found*' [III ii 133–4], and the destruction so wrought exacts a penance as deep as it is prolonged, making the sixteen-year gap in the action an integral part of the countervailing restorative process. Youth *v.* Age is echoed again in Polixenes' angry reaction to Florizel's proposed match with Perdita [IV iv 414ff.] and is anticipated in the flowers that Perdita distributes to her various guests. In the scene that narrates the revelation of Perdita's true parentage Leontes is described as simultaneously beside himself 'for joy of his found daughter', yet echoing the past in begging Bohemia's forgiveness, and seeming to renew his loss in his cries of 'O, thy mother, thy mother!' Meanwhile, the Old Shepherd, as if ranging the whole gamut of time, 'stands by like a weather-bitten conduit of many kings' reigns' [v ii 48–54]. In the climactic following scene the statue, though a remarkable likeness of Hermione, strikes Leontes as too aged, which prompts in Paulina the adroit, but also thematically appropriate, explanation,

> So much the more our carver's excellence,
> Which lets go by some sixteen years and makes her
> As she lived now.   [v iii 30–2]

As Professor Ewbank comments, 'The whole scene has about it a sense of the fulness of time' ('The Triumph of Time', p. 97); and the final coming to life of the statue is a symbolic filling of the grave [v iii 101] dug by Time, the agent of destruction, as he converts into the agent of reunion and renewal.

There is thus a constant sense of relationships developing and changing with time, out of which develops awareness of the existence of a natural bond linking the generations and ultimately sustaining life in spite of all that is done to disrupt and uproot it. Accordingly, when Time speaks as Chorus in IV i he does not break the sequence of the play, but only projects, though admittedly in a more explicitly allegorical form than is characteristic of the rest of the play, something which is implicitly there throughout its general texture. His action, as he says, is both creative and destructive: he pleases some and tries all; is 'both joy and terror / Of good and bad'; and 'makes and unfolds error' [1–2]. His language is filled with the sense of things both flourishing and decaying, and, in particular, he is the embodiment of the concept of 'growth'. 'Impute it not a crime', he says, that he slides over sixteen years and leaves 'the growth untried / Of that wide gap' [4, 6–7]; with the audience's patience he gives his 'scene such growing / As you had slept between' [16–17]; and he speaks of Perdita as 'now grown in grace / Equal with wond'ring' [24–5]. The emphasis is thus on organic processes, and this is echoed elsewhere in the many references to growth and natural development [e.g. I i 23–4; II ii

59–61, iii 12–17, 89–90, 103–4; iii i 1–2; iv iv 79–103, 115–16, 131–2, 549–51; v i 150–1]. Death and life are both embraced and seen ultimately as parts of one beneficently continuous whole.

The structure of the play may therefore be seen as based on the opposition between, but final reconciliation of, destructive and creative, tragic and comic halves – its two-part structure being marked by the midway intervention of Time; and, though Jacobean performances probably ran through from beginning to end without a break, in modern productions the obvious point at which to make an interval would seem to be at the end of Act iii. In terms of the play's inner meaning, however, the change comes in the middle of iii iii, where the tragic phase reaches its culmination in the exposure of Perdita, but is modulated into comedy by the Old Shepherd's taking-up the child and the Clown's grotesque account of the deaths of Antigonus and the sailors. Here the organic process of continuity rather than abrupt reversal is given dramatic realisation through the tonal metamorphosis of the scene and the skilful control of the audience's response. The prominence given to Time by his appearance as Chorus in iv i still remains, but it is absorbed into the larger sense of things dying and growing which gives the play its overall unity. When it is seen in this perspective the structure is three-part rather than two, corresponding to the changing of place from Sicilia to Bohemia and back to Sicilia again. The basis of this structure is both seasonal (once again echoing the play's title) and social: its first movement belongs to winter and the Court and is essentially destructive; its second movement, which combines spring and summer, belongs to the countryside and is alive with a counterbalancing creative vitality; and its final movement, which may be seen as autumnal, bears the fruit of Leontes' repentance and brings the reviving energy of the countryside and youth to effect the regeneration of the Court. Each movement has its pivotal centre (in the first, the trial scene; in the second, the sheep-shearing festival; and in the third, the animation of the statue) which satisfyingly matches thematic change to dramatic spectacle, and all three are bound together in the interlocking harmony of the play's 'growth'.

3   WINTER: LEONTES' JEALOUSY

The 'winter' of the play is created by Leontes' jealousy, and its
context is the Court of Sicily. The play opens, however, with an
emphasis on courtliness which is not at all sinister and an
atmosphere quite free from the suggestion of jealousy. In i i
Camillo and Archidamus echo in their own words and
behaviour the complete amity and mutual esteem which exists
between their respective masters, and Camillo emphasises the
deep-rooted continuity of their friendship: 'They were trained
together in their childhoods: and there rooted betwixt them
such an affection, which cannot choose but branch now'
[22–4]. Although it has been argued that the verb 'branch' has
ominous overtones hinting at a fall from this harmonious state,
the more reasonable interpretation is to see it as simply an
extension of the planting and development of the tree of
friendship which is metaphorically implicit in the first half of
the sentence. The accent is on a kind of fertile harmony, and it is
followed quite naturally by an allusion to the next generation in
the person of the 'young prince Mamillius' [34], through whom
the innocent boyhood friendship of the two kings receives
renewal, and in whom there is the embodiment of that healthy
power of nature which 'physics the subject, makes old hearts
fresh' [37–8].

The larger courtly ensemble of i ii is also characterised by
ceremonious formality and is, initially at least, equally un-
tainted. Polixenes' rhetoric may be playfully over-elaborate,
but, even if Hermione comes on stage in a condition of obvious
pregnancy (and it is debatable whether the text supports this),
it is too discordant with i i for this to be presented as a hint
(along with the supposed ambiguity of such words as 'burden'
and 'multiply') that Polixenes might be considered the father of
her expected child. Such an interpretation implies the injection
of meaning into Polixenes' words of which he himself is
unconscious, and it requires the audience to grasp that Leontes
is already distorting what he hears – which, as a matter of
practical theatre, is absurd.

For the first eighty-six lines Leontes has little to say, and this
might encourage a director who is intent on finding signs of

very early jealousy to present him as half-hearted in his desire
to have Polixenes stay longer; but there is nothing in what he
does to suggest hostility. The less questionable assumption is
that Leontes is sincere, and that he asks for Hermione's
assistance because he instinctively relies on her and trusts in
her influence as a hostess. Hermione speaks only because she is
asked to, and in a tone that echoes the established atmosphere
of warm friendliness. What can be said, however, is that the
unguarded freedom of her chatter with Polixenes leaves her
husband free to become conscious of his own lack of success and
feel a tinge of envy poisoning his sense of her motives. The
result is that when he rejoins the conversation a cloud has
passed over his mental heaven. The aside, 'At my request he
would not' [87], signals this change to the audience; and from
now on words that have borne only one – and that an essentially
innocent – meaning, take on a jealous ambiguity.

If there are words prior to this moment which might be
ascribed a double value – signifying, that is to say, one thing for
the speaker, but something over and above that for the
audience – they may perhaps be found in Polixenes' speech
evoking his childhood friendship with Leontes [67–75]. This is
a continuation and elaboration of Camillo's earlier words to
Archidamus, and its primary function is to strengthen the
impression of an innocent, unsullied relationship which has all
the freshness and vitality of youth. It also develops, however,
into a comment on the inevitability of the loss of innocence
which has theological overtones, making the audience conscious of the Fall of Man in a specifically sexual context, and to
that extent ready for the lapse which is to come. And it is also
possible, as Dover Wilson suggests in a note to the New
Cambridge edition, that Leontes, who has moved up stage
during this speech, rejoins his wife and friend just in time to
hear, without understanding their connection with what has
gone before, Hermione's joking words on sexual 'sin':

> Th'offences we have made you do we'll answer,
> If you first sinned with us, and that with us
> You did continue fault, and that you slipped not
> With any but with us.   [83–6]

Being unaware that 'we' has its antecedent in 'Your queen and
I' at line 82, Leontes might therefore be conceived as mistaking
it for a use of the royal 'we', referring to Hermione alone, and
thus gain the impression she means adultery with Polixenes.
Such an interpretation adds accidental ambiguity to the
passage, and might well commend itself to some directors as a
useful way of increasing the plausibility of Leontes' jealousy. It
is, however, a somewhat mechanical device, unlike the subtler
poetic effect of Polixenes' allusion to the Fall.

Another approach is to assume that Leontes is jealous before
the play begins – that the jealousy is a *donnée* equivalent to the
fairy-story formula, 'Once upon a time there was a King who
was jealous. . . .' The difficulty here is that the audience must
appreciate that Leontes' opening remarks are ironical, without
the help of any clear indication in the dialogue. Alternatively,
the actor must speak with a bitterness sufficiently strong to
make the point clear to the audience, but without the characters on stage seeming to notice it. Either way, the theatrical
situation is unduly strained, and the theme of a fall from
innocence is deprived of its appropriate embodiment in the
play's action.

The assumption best supported by the text, and quite
workable in theatrical terms, is that the first certain note of
sourness, indicating a change of consciousness in Leontes,
comes at line 87. The dialogue which then follows between
Leontes and Hermione involves a counterpointing of her
continued gaiety against the apparent sharing of her mood on
Leontes' part, but with an undertone which betrays his now
sardonic inner meaning. Thus he appears to congratulate her
on her success with Polixenes by saying that she never spoke to
better purpose but once, and when she asks to know what that
'once' was he replies,

> Why that was when
> Three crabbèd months had soured themselves to death
> Ere I could make thee open thy white hand
> And clap thyself my love . . . .   [101–4]

'Crabbèd', 'soured' and 'death' give the natural anxiety of
courtship a bitterness that is obviously excessive. Hermione

may or may not react to it, but in any case she does not allow it
to change her mood. The Folio text has no stage direction, but
most editors, reasonably in view of Leontes' 'Too hot, too
hot! . . .' [108], assume that she takes Polixenes' hand and
engages in conversation with him, while Leontes speaks the
first soliloquy of the play, to himself or to the audience. The
function of this soliloquy is to let the audience understand the
inner change that is coming over Leontes. It is true that there is
no Iago here to generate a plausible process of growing
suspicion and to feed Leontes' mind, as Iago so cunningly feeds
Othello's, with partially presented 'evidence' of his wife's
supposed infidelity; but enough is done to create an adequate
impression in the theatre of a man who, while seeing what
others see, is beginning to view things suspiciously, and, as
lines 110–11 suggest, is being thrown by his emotion into a state
of physical agitation. The turmoil grows before the audience's
eyes. The normal sense of what Hermione's conduct means is
still present to Leontes' mind in lines 111–14 (he recognises
that it may 'well become the agent'), but the 'paddling palms
and pinching fingers' of his subsequent description show him
painting her and Polixenes' actions with a colouring that comes
from his now-sickening mind. It is not the detached language of
observation, but that of compulsive denigration and sexual
revulsion; and its culmination in 'O, that is entertainment / My
bosom likes not, nor my brows' [118–19] marks the surfacing of
jealousy in a bitter variation on the stale horns/cuckoldry joke.
The audience, of course, are free to judge Hermione and
Polixenes' conduct for themselves, and a director may choose to
include actions which provide more or less support to Leontes'
interpretation; but it would be a singularly perverse production
that did not make the distorting effect of Leontes' subjective
view apparent.

The next phase in the development of Leontes' jealousy
significantly involves his relationship with his son, Mamillius.
He emerges from his soliloquy to speak to the child, and the
language of fatherly affection – action, too, if, as is probable, he
wipes the boy's nose – underlines the link between a capacity
for playfulness and the fresh, restorative power of youth. The
by-play, however, between father and child mirrors the
struggle between normality and tragic abnormality in Leontes'

changing consciousness. He cannot give Mamillius his undi-
vided attention; his eye keeps straying from his son to his wife
and Polixenes, and even in his dialogue with Mamillius his
words, through a process of pejorative word-play, deteriorate
into salacity. Thus at line 123 'neat' loses its 'cleanly' meaning
to become 'neat' in the sense of 'horned cattle', with sinister
sexual overtones; at line 126 it temporarily recovers its better
meaning through the affectionate liveliness of 'wanton calf!';
but at lines 128–9 it is again associated with cuckoldry.
Moreover most of this passes over the boy's head; Leontes'
language turns inward, ceasing to be a means of communica-
tion between himself and his son, and poisoning even his
delight in their physical resemblance. As if realising the harm
he is doing, he tries to pull himself back into a true relationship
with his son by means of familiar endearments such as 'Most
dear'st! My collop!', but his attempt is shattered by an abrupt
and completely destabilising jerk of attention back to the
supposed treachery of his wife:

> Can thy dam? May't be?
> Affection, thy intention stabs the centre.
> Thou dost make possible things not so held,
> Communicat'st with dreams – how can this be? –
> With what's unreal thou coactive art,
> And fellow'st nothing. [137–42]

Here the obscurity of the language is deliberate, and in
dramatic terms also highly effective. It removes Leontes into a
solipsistic world, which paradoxically makes the impossible
seem possible and has its intercourse with dreams, yet forms
relationship with nothing. The would-be interchange between
father and child collapses; and, in parallel with it, the adult
relationship with wife and friend also collapses – a fact
underlined by Polixenes' and Hermione's awareness of his
withdrawn, distracted state [146–50]. Leontes attempts to
cover this up by saying that he was preoccupied with thoughts
of his own childhood prompted by looking on Mamillius's face.
The effect, however, of this re-creation of the child's world is
only to emphasise his loss, and he is soon dismissing his son in
his next soliloquy with a riot of imagery that converts true

playfulness into a preoccupation with the false playing –
indeed, play-acting – which he imagines his wife to be engaged
in with Polixenes, and which involves himself in 'so disgraced a
part, whose issue / Will hiss me to my grave' [188–9].

As the soliloquy progresses it becomes increasingly a one-
man show in which relationship with another real person has
no place, and in which Leontes creates a jaundiced satirical
comedy of marital infidelity, with himself cast in the major role
of deceived husband. Couched in language of wilful vulgarity
('sluiced', 'bawdy planet', 'No barricado for a belly') it
becomes a travesty of the play's true action, while yet being a
startling revelation of Leontes' tragic immersion in a drama of
his own devising. Here, as elsewhere in *The Winter's Tale*,
Shakespeare comes perilously near to exposing the thinness of
the bounds which divide reality from unreality, and deliberately exploits the audience's awareness of their own situation
as spectators of an artificially contrived entertainment. But the
result is not to trivialise what they see before them. By being
made more conscious of the mimetic function of the drama they
gain greater insight into the distorting effect of Leontes' jealous
imagination. His fantasy world parodies rather than holds the
mirror up to the natural world; it represents a lost capacity to
distinguish properly between the two. He can now only believe
in the play created in his mind; and all referential standards
collapse as he ceases to communicate with the real Mamillius
and then formally dismisses him from the stage. Thereafter
father and son are never seen together again (Mamillius's one
other appearance is with his mother in II i). The playful
relationship between them deteriorates into a corrupt version
of playing which proves destructive, not creative, culminating
in the father's outrageous treatment of the mother, which
virtually kills the son.

In its full-blown condition Leontes' jealousy becomes a
disease. He sees himself as infected by the disease of cuckoldry
in common with other unsuspecting husbands – 'Many
thousands on's / Have the disease and feel't not' [206–7]; and
in his lengthy dialogue with Camillo, after the dismissal of
Mamillius, he attempts to impose his own diseased outlook on
the man who has been the soundest of his advisers. Normal
sanity speaks out in the latter's 'Good my lord, be cured / Of

this diseased opinion' [296–7], but to Leontes such truth is only
a lie. It is 'diseased opinion' which triumphs over health, and
Camillo is forced to temporise to save his own life and that of
Polixenes. He remains essentially true, rejecting obedience to
'one / Who in rebellion with himself, will have / All that are his
so too' [354–6]; but even in the words with which he seeks to
warn Polixenes of his danger there is a reflection of the diseased
inversion which Leontes has imposed on all around him:

> There is a sickness
> Which puts some of us in distemper, but
> I cannot name the disease; and it is caught
> Of you, that yet are well.   [384–7]

The riddle is sorted out, but the impression left with the
audience is that Leontes' jealousy has become so contagious a
disease that for health and normality flight from the Court is
inevitable.

4   WINTER: THE DESTRUCTION OF INNOCENCE

By the beginning of Act II Leontes' 'diseased opinion' is thus
firmly established. The audience are given one last reminder of
healthier conditions in the playful scene between the now-
certainly pregnant Hermione and Mamillius, but only to
heighten the destructiveness which is to follow when Leontes
peremptorily orders the separation of son and mother. This
creates a vivid dramatic image of the deprivation of family
relationship which he is in the process of inflicting on himself;
and the effect is curiously mirrored when Antigonus attempts
to show the strength of his belief in the Queen by declaring
that he will 'geld' his own daughters if she is 'honour-
flawed':

> Fourteen they shall not see
> To bring false generations. They are co-heirs;
> And I had rather glib myself than they
> Should not produce fair issue.   [II i 147–50]

Such violence of language, however, betrays the corruption that has infected him and the other courtiers, even though it has not completely blinded his judgement. Antigonus cannot function as Hermione's true champion. That role is assigned to his wife, Paulina – a character whose tone and manner, devoid of courtly compliment, suggests that she is in the Court, but not of it. Her indignation at finding the Queen imprisoned –

> Good lady,
> No court in Europe is too good for thee:
> What dost thou then in prison?   [II ii 2–4]

– implies a standard of moral worth far transcending mere courtliness, and a use of the conventional Court/prison contrast to emphasise the reversal of sane values expressed in Hermione's situation. Moreover, she is equally outspoken in the presence of Leontes. The male courtiers, though not obsequious, are too anxious to humour him as much as they can; but Paulina's bluntness creates a much more vigorous sense of resistance to his violation of natural principles. Likewise, her spontaneous offer to take the new-born child out of the prison and carry it to the Court shows her forthrightness in translating belief into action. Once there she characteristically brushes the courtiers aside; and to the Servant's fearful plea that 'he hath not slept tonight, commanded / None should come at him' she makes a sharp retort which puts 'sleep' and the restorative power of the innocent child in true perspective:

> I come to bring him sleep. 'Tis such as you,
> That creep like shadows by him, and do sigh
> At each his needless heavings – such as you
> Nourish the cause of his awaking. I
> Do come with words as med'cinal as true,
> Honest as either, to purge him of that humour
> That presses him from sleep.   [II iii 32–9]

There is a touch of traditional comedy (going back at least to Noah's wife in the miracle plays) in Paulina's role as the scolding termagant whom her husband cannot control; but that is not allowed to undercut the value of her demonstration of a loyalty which, like that of Kent in *King Lear*, shows itself in healthy criticism of the King rather than flattery that will only encourage his disease. The very noise she creates as she makes the theatre echo with her defiance is at once occasion for laughter and an effective dramatic expression of her significance as truth-teller; and its fitting climax is her bold proffering of the child itself, coupled with repeated insistence on the 'goodness' of the Queen:

> The good Queen –
> For she is good – hath brought you forth a daughter:
> Here 'tis; commends it to your blessing.   [64–6]

The battle of words that subsequently develops between Paulina and Leontes continues the vein of comedy, as is very noticeable when the scene is played in the theatre; but it also has its more serious implications. There is even a sense in which Paulina's outspokenness contributes to the tragic consequence, for her reiteration of the close resemblance between the father and the child exacerbates Leontes' anger to the point where he orders not only that she be pushed out of doors, but also that the child be burnt to death; and it takes the prostration of all the courtiers to make him change his doom to one of exposure in 'some remote and desert place, quite out / Of our dominions' [175–6]. Not that this diminishes Paulina's stand. Her dispute with Leontes is the dramatised encounter of selfless energy in the cause of natural innocence with selfish violence intent on the destruction of its own 'issue'; and this also has an ultimately beneficial consequence, for, as so often in cases of extreme opposition, their preoccupation with each other hints at a kind of relationship which draws them together, as will be seen in the final movement of the play.

In the meantime, however, Leontes remains fixed in his jealous distortion, the climax of which is his subjection of Hermione to a supposedly judicial process which, for him, is to be merely a confirmation of her guilt. The role of sane discrimination here shifts from Paulina to the Queen herself. It is she, with her dignity and calm reasonableness, who dominates the trial scene; though the defence she offers is one based on her emotional situation rather than legal arguments. Given the one-sided nature of Leontes' accusations, there is little scope for debate or cross-examination: as Hermione says, 'My life stands in the level of your dreams' [III ii 80]. All she can do is to insist on her character as a chaste and loyal wife and queen, placed in singularly humiliating circumstances, and – in the words of Helen Faucit, a nineteenth-century actress of the part – having 'him for her accuser who should best have known how her whole nature belied his accusation' (quoted in Variorum edn, p. 117). In presenting such a case she is given words that again show Shakespeare's willingness – so marked in this play – to make use of the physical context of the theatre. This is a scene 'devised / And played to take spectators' [35–6], and Hermione's exposure ''fore / Who please to come and hear' [40–1] gives her humiliation the double-take of an appeal both to the stage audience of the trial and to the actual audience of the play, which daringly combines the sense of outrage with the sense of spectacle. The result, however, is not devaluation of the performance, but an effective heightening of its emotional and moral potentiality.

The same may be said of the pomp and ceremony associated with the oracle. It provides opportunities for theatrical splendour, which can be (and have been) abused, but which, properly handled, have great dramatic force. The oracle is a focus for the intimations of a controlling destiny which permeate the play. Its almost religious significance is underlined by the brief scene [III i] in which Cleomenes and Dion express their feelings of awe at Delphos, and this is reinforced by their solemn oath at the trial that its message has come direct from the hand of Apollo's priest. The occasion thus provided for heightening the dramatic tension is essential to the conflict between destruction and creation which is now reaching its greatest intensity; and to lessen the effect by omitting III i, as some directors do, is certainly a mistake. Apollo stands for divinely sanctioned truth; and when his judgement is revealed, completely exculpating Hermione and giving Leontes' treatment of his own child such ominous meaning, the collective release of tension – 'Now blessed be the great Apollo!' [III ii 134] – seems complete. But the strength of Leontes' obstinate perversity in fact screws the tension still higher; and, if the atmosphere has been built up in the way the text demands, his crude denunciation, 'There is no truth at all i'th'oracle!' [136], bursts upon the audience as a piece of

outrageous blasphemy. The immediately following news of
Mamillius's death then seems to come as instant and catas-
trophic retribution, or at least it is so interpreted by Leontes:
'Apollo's angry, and the heavens themselves / Do strike at my
injustice' [144–5]; and the collapse of Hermione prompts
Paulina to the cry, 'This news is mortal to the Queen: look
down / And see what death is doing' [146–7].

This is the absolute climax of the play's wintry movement.
The King has virtually destroyed his own family and left
himself, and the state also, with no possibility of continuity. He
immediately repents, making a speech which acknowledges his
'great profaneness', and declares his willingness to reconcile
himself with Polixenes, 'new woo' his queen, and recall
Camillo; but such quick relenting is suspiciously superficial.
His command (presumably to Paulina and the ladies) to carry
Hermione off the stage indicates a comparatively trivial view of
her condition – ('Her heart is but o'ercharged; she will recover'
[148]. Much more than this is needed to counterbalance the
devastation he has caused. Hence the extravagance of Paulina's language when she makes her seemingly melodramatic
re-entrance. Her speech, with its near-hysterical string of
questions,

> What studied torments, tyrant, hast for me?
> What wheels? Racks? Fires? What flaying? Boiling
> In leads or oils?   [173–5]

and almost garish rehearsal of the sins Leontes has committed,
is a means by which her own grief and rage may find release;
but, more to the point dramatically, it emphasises the enormity
of what has been done, and prolongs its tragic reverberation.
Appropriately, it reiterates, and culminates again in, the theme
of death – though now not the death of the son, but of the Queen
from whose womb that son has been born, as if re-creation itself
has now been destroyed. At least death is what it seems to be.
Paulina is emphatic that it is so, and the audience are given no
hints that it might be otherwise. One possible view of Paulina's
histrionic behaviour is that she is deliberately over-acting; but,
if so, nothing is actually done or said to leave either the
courtiers on the stage or the audience in the theatre with the
impression that Hermione still lives.

Perhaps at this moment Paulina herself believes that the Queen is dead; and perhaps when she later discovers that this is not so, she manages to persuade Hermione that it is better to keep her survival a secret till Leontes' remorse has wrought a deep and lasting change in him. Perhaps – but this is mere speculation. There is no justification for it in the text, and it cannot be said to exist as any sort of theatrical reality for the audience of the play at this point in its revelation through performance. As of this dramatic moment the Queen is effectively dead. Destruction has done its worst; and the full force of this has to be brought home to Leontes.

In dramatic terms this must also be the justification for the otherwise curious extravagance of Paulina's injunction to Leontes not to repent, but to betake himself to despair, and for the appalling bleakness of her Job's comfort in telling him that

> A thousand knees,
> Ten thousand years together, naked, fasting,
> Upon a barren mountain, and still winter
> In storm perpetual, could not move the gods
> To look that way thou wert.   [208–12]

The excessiveness implicit in these words is acknowledged by Paulina in her next speech [216–30], but they strike the essential note, to which Leontes is now more ready to respond than he would be to courtly tact. They express the spiritual winter that he has made of his life and the completion of the tragedy in which he has been the protagonist. Accordingly, the scene – and the play's first movement – ends with Leontes in a posture of penitence that is unqualified, and which he envisages as lasting for the rest of his life. It is a penitence, however, performed for its own sake, without belief that it will win him any kind of compensation. The one word that may ambiguously carry a more positive suggestion is 'recreation', used in connection with the ritual of remorse which Leontes vows to undertake:

> Once a day, I'll visit
> The chapel where they lie, and tears shed there
> Shall be my recreation.   [236–8]

As J. H. P. Pafford comments, 'The word contains the sense of *diversion* or refreshment but also that of restoration, re-creation of the spirit' (Arden edn, p. 66). The first of these two meanings has its relationship to the playfulness with which *The Winter's Tale* began, but which Leontes has perverted into destruction. In his own consciousness the word is primarily ironic – such 'recreation', thanks to the havoc wreaked by his own inordinate jealousy, is the only kind of play that is now left him to enjoy. In the consciousness of the audience it might stir the second meaning, and so hint at a more creative outcome. But, if so, the suggestion is, at most, subdued and remote. The final words of the scene, and, appropriately, the last to be heard from Leontes till his distant reappearance in v i, are those on which he makes his exit: 'Come, / And lead me to these sorrows' [240–1]. The note they sound is one of resignation to, and acceptance of, grief. If they suggest any sort of beginning, it is the beginning only of Leontes' recognition of the tragic consequences of his actions.

5   SPRING–SUMMER: THE SHEEP-SHEARING FESTIVAL

The role of Time as Chorus in IV i has already been discussed (*see above*, p. 13). He bridges the years between one movement and the next with a subtle emphasis on the timelessness, yet temporal continuity, over which he presides, and he turns the audience's mind away from the inward-looking, arrested grief of Leontes to the new, expansive characters whom he 'names' to them as 'Florizel' (a prince of romance, with obvious 'floral' overtones) and 'Perdita' ('the lost one'). The work of effecting a transition from 'winter' to 'spring', however, has already been assisted by the scene at the conclusion of Act III in which the child is exposed and discovered by the Old Shepherd. There tragedy and comedy meet. Its first half is an extension of the destructive movement, reaching its culmination in the deaths of Antigonus and the sailors, accompanied by storm (a recurrent symbol in Shakespeare for tragic disorder) and the cacophonous din of the bear hunt. In the second half the child is rescued from death; and the contrast with what has preceded is clearly signalled by the words of the Shepherd to his son: 'Now bless thyself; thou met'st with things dying, I with things new-born' [III iii 109–10]. But there is no simple, stark antithesis. The change from comedy to tragedy is graduated, and elements of each mood infiltrate both halves of the scene. Antigonus's soliloquy, for example, borders at moments on burlesque (as in the histrionic language associated with his distorted vision of Hermione: 'gasping to begin some speech, her eyes / Became two spouts' and 'with shrieks, / She melted into air' [24–5, 35–6]; and the manner of his death, conveyed in the notorious stage direction *'Exit, pursued by a bear'*, poses fascinating problems for a director. Antigonus's own comment, 'This is the chase' [56], suggests a comic reversal of human–hunter and animal–quarry; and the bringing of a bear on stage (it is absent from the source material) suggests that Shakespeare is once again playing on the theatricality of his theatrical devices, with an ambiguous attitude towards the seriousness of the effect. The episode is tragic, comic, melo-dramatic, farcical – all at once. Similarly, in the second half the emphasis is on cheerfulness and new life, but in the Shepherd's typically old man's view of brawling, mugging, girl-chasing youth [58–64] there is a combination of energy and destructive violence with playing for laughs that blurs the distinction between genres. And his linguistic confusion (a well-established convention with such characters in Shakespearean comedy as Bottom and Dogberry and Verges) in the statement, 'If thou'lt see a thing to talk on when thou art dead and rotten, come hither' [78–9], takes the sting out of death. Above all, the Clown's speech alternating Antigonus's pursuit by the bear with the drowning of the sailors becomes a brilliant exercise in the tragi-comic grotesque: 'how the poor souls roared, and the sea mocked them; how the poor gentleman roared, and the bear mocked him, both roaring louder than the sea or weather' [96–8]. Yet the effect is not one of heartlessness. The violence is distanced without sympathy being lost; and the old man and his son do deeds of charity. By the time this scene is finished the audience are aware that they have joined the world of reassuringly absurd characters. It has modulated like a piece of music from minor to major key, and a new movement has begun.

Newness is also felt in the appearance of a quite unexpected character. The way has been prepared for Florizel and Perdita, yet the figure who now bursts upon the audience is the attractive, but disconcerting, Autolycus. As J. H. P. Pafford remarks, 'in so far as Autolycus is a thief, a pick-pocket, and a cheat, he could, in the study, be unpleasant. . . . On the stage the crimes of Autolycus are hardly felony at all' (Arden edn, p. lxxx). He is a courtier fallen from grace, turned con-man and petty thief; his name means 'All-wolf, Very-wolf, Wolf's-self' (Variorum edn, p. 3); and he owes a good deal to the 'Conny-catching' pamphlets in which Robert Greene exposed the swindling tricks of the Elizabethan underworld. The chief source, however, is probably Ovid's *Metamorphoses*, where he is mentioned as the son of a mortal mother, Chione, and Mercury (god of thieves), and half-brother of Philammon, whose father was Apollo. This relationship may well account for his appearance at this moment instead of Florizel, for, different as he and the prince appear to be, they are linked by the common metamorphoses of disguise and their associations with Mercury and Apollo respectively. When Florizel does make his entrance [IV iv] he comes in disguised as a shepherd, and, in a passage which sounds almost like an allusion to Ovid, he compares his own situation with the 'transformations' of Jupiter and Neptune and, more specifically, 'the fire-robed god, / Golden Apollo' who also became 'a poor, humble swain, / As I seem now' [29–31]. Autolycus makes his entrance [IV iii] in the form of a tinker, and he announces that he was 'littered under Mercury'. He soon pretends to be a traveller who has been stripped and robbed and left with nothing but disgusting rags; and in IV iv he turns up again disguised as a pedlar. When Camillo devises the plan for the flight from Bohemia, Florizel and Autolycus acquire still further forms of disguise through their exchange of clothes, and this enables Autolycus to play his old courtier role, at least in the eyes of the Old Shepherd and his son. Thus he and Florizel become curiously connected: their common experience of 'transformations' hints at a transforming power at work in the play, and they both break through convention and conformity to bring fresh, natural vitality into a tragically jaded world.

However, there is nothing merely pretty or sentimental in

this new vigour and energy. Although Autolycus enters singing (paradoxically, an Apollonian gift), his song aptly reflects his carelessly amoral character. It celebrates the triumph of 'the red blood' of spring over the 'pale' complexion of winter, but its references to 'doxy' and 'pugging' fuse prostitution and theft with 'the sweet o' the year' indifferently. He is predatory, sensual, cheerful and self-indulgent, all at once. As S. L. Bethel comments, the primary importance of the song is 'in bringing the ideal world of romance into unmistakable relation with contemporary life, even in its less savoury aspects' ('*The Winter's Tale': A Study*, p. 46). Even more important, though, is the impression it gives of cocking a snook at guilt and conscience, especially after the earlier scenes of Leontes' jealousy and the remorse to which it leads. Autolycus is frank about his crimes and cowardice, and cares not a fig for moral retribution: 'For the life to come, I sleep out the thought of it' [IV iii 29–30]. In that, like Falstaff, he captures the anarchic sympathies of the audience. Although they may not approve, he touches the irresponsibility within them which is also a source of vitality; and to enter with a song which is paradoxically both life-affirming and vicious is to make an immediately recognisable and fundamental appeal which is irresistible.

The mood of the song flows over into the action with Autolycus's trick of pretending to be robbed and beaten in order to gain the Clown's sympathy and pick his pocket in the process. There is no stage direction in the Folio, but tradition – going back at least as far as the eighteenth-century editor Capell – has Autolycus's theft take place between his double moan of 'Softly, dear sir' and 'good sir, softly', thus lending a comic ambiguity to 'You ha' done me a charitable office' [75] and to his following pretence of pained virtue in refusing the Clown's offer of money – 'Offer me no money, I pray you: that kills my heart' [81–2]. The joke of knowing and not knowing increases when Autolycus gives his attacker his own name [97], and by so doing elicits an unwitting condemnation of himself in the Clown's reply, 'Not a more cowardly rogue in all Bohemia. If you had but looked big and spit at him, he'd have run' [102–3]. Autolycus's character is thus accurately presented, but in circumstances that enable him to establish the co-median's favourite posture of collusive intimacy with the audience. That is, he is essentially a *stage* figure – as much so as a pantomime dame; and, though Shakespeare avoids the sentimentality that usually goes with pantomime, he gives Autolycus the same privilege as the dame enjoys, of playing his part within the dramatised situation while striking up a special relationship with the audience. To this extent, Autolycus makes a unique contribution to the spring–summer movement. As a result of his appearance it is marked not only by changes in style, place and theme (and, of course, the advent of new characters), but also by an even more striking change of theatrical rhythm. A new sense of aliveness permeates the drama, emanating from a new sense of relationship between actor and audience, which seems to release a hitherto untapped source of energy and vigour.

The concentrated centre of this energy is the sheep-shearing festival of IV iv. Florizel and Perdita quickly establish themselves as hero and heroine in a dramatised pastoral which nevertheless has a complexity of levels unprecedented in pastoral literature, except for Shakespeare's own *As You Like It*. They are themselves and not themselves, as indicated by the emphasis on 'transformations' already noted. Their metamorphosis onto a level of mythical transcendence is playfully alluded to by Florizel when he calls Perdita 'no shepherdess, but Flora / Peering in April's front' and her sheep-shearing 'a meeting of the petty gods', with herself 'the queen on't' [2–5]. This enthusiastic hyperbole is becoming to him as an enraptured young lover, and it rises to lyrical intensity in his speech at lines 135–46 evoking Perdita's natural grace as the expression of innate royalty:

> Each your doing,
> So singular in each particular,
> Crowns what you are doing in the present deeds,
> That all your acts are queens.   [143–6]

That such a response is not merely the dazzled effect of love is confirmed by Polixenes' 'nothing she does or seems / But smacks of something greater than herself' [157–8] and Camillo's 'she is / The queen of curds and cream' [160–1]; but Perdita is far from forgetting the social implications of the situation in which Florizel's 'high self' is 'obscured / With a swain's wearing', and she herself, 'poor lowly maid', is 'Most goddess-like pranked up' [7–10]. The idealised pastoral is thus kept in touch with the political realities of the situation. Likewise, their conventionally pure love – Florizel is emphatic that his 'desires / Run not before [his] honour' [33–4] – is also passionate, and far from sexless. Perdita in particular is not a merely symbolic figure, but an individualised girl with strong natural feelings. In her debate with Polixenes [79–103] she rejects his orthodox argument that Art may combine with Nature to produce an art which 'itself is Nature', upholding instead the uncompromised vigour of 'great creating Nature'. The corollary of this is that she totally accepts the physical, reproductive basis of love; and when she strews Florizel with flowers 'burying' (with its overtones of the death-oriented action of the 'winter' movement) is converted into a creative enactment of love, like the planting of seed in the ground: 'Not like a corpse; or if, not to be buried, / But quick and in mine arms' [131–2].

The lyricism of IV iv is most evident in the speeches with which Perdita accompanies her distribution of flowers. By making them appropriate to the maturity of the recipients she reinforces the dramatic substance of the scene, which includes characters of all ages, and recapitulates the thematic variety of the play through all the seasons (for instance, winter, 75; autumn, 79–80; summer, 107; spring, 113). But the lyrical is not the scene's only mode. A different fashion of doing things is vividly described by the Old Shepherd when he recalls the domestic hustling and jollity of his dead wife's manner of playing the hostess, by comparison with which, he thinks, Perdita is too 'retired' [55–62]. This still has its equivalent in the present, however – for example, in the uninhibited rusticity of the Clown, Mopsa and Dorcas and the entertainments they favour, which provide a crude, but striking, counterpoint to the natural dignity and instinctive refinement of Perdita. There are other contrasts, too. As a balance to Perdita's singing, which Florizel so admires that he tells her,

> when you sing,
> I'd have you buy and sell so, so give alms,
> Pray so, and, for the ord'ring your affairs,
> To sing them too   [137–40]

there is the re-entry of Autolycus and his singing of the perfect ad-man's song to get his customers to 'come buy, come buy' [220–31]; and the practical demonstration he gives of his wares when he joins with Mopsa and Dorcas in a three-part ballad of gawdy sexual rivalry, which matches the dramatic situation on stage between these two girls and the Clown (it goes, appropriately, 'to the tune of "Two maids wooing a man" ' [287]. Again, on the exalted, imaginative level there is the dancing, which Florizel conceives as a perfect example of Perdita's gracefulness:

> when you do dance, I wish you
> A wave o'th'sea, that you might ever do
> Nothing but that – move still, still so,
> And own no other function. [140–3]

In actual performance there is the *'dance of Shepherds and Shepherdesses'*, which is probably a ring dance called a 'brawl' or 'branle' (Alan Brissenden, *Shakespeare and the Dance*, p. 89); and, in marked contrast to both of these, there is the dance performed by 'three carters, three shepherds, three neat-herds, three swine-herds, that have made themselves all men of hair' – a satyrs' dance rough enough, and crude enough, to require a preliminary apology. The scene's pastoral refinement, is thus (like Autolycus's first song) deliberately connected to other areas of experience which might seem to have an alien vulgarity and coarseness, but which are equally important expressions of the new life celebrated in 'spring'. The sheep-shearing becomes a real country festival, and its entertainments those of a robust, and even primitive, rusticity. The effect, however, is not to deflate the lyrical idealism, or reduce it to burlesque, but to strengthen it by joining it to a living popular tradition.

6   SPRING–SUMMER: THE AFFIRMATION OF 'REASON'

The complex interaction between high and low styles which is the substance of the sheep-shearing festival is seriously challenged, yet survives that challenge, when Polixenes decides that the idyll shared by Perdita and Florizel must be shattered. He makes his first move by suggesting that Florizel is not generous enough in buying 'knacks' for Perdita, only to receive the idealistic reply that she 'prizes not such trifles as these are' and wants only gifts that belong to the heart [IV iv 354–6]; but Florizel's subsequently hyperbolic declaration of love, and willingness to dispense with his father's consent to his intended marriage, precipitates the revelation that the man he is speaking to is that very father, the King himself. With melodramatic, but effective, rhetoric, Florizel's 'Mark our contract' then becomes Polixenes' 'Mark your divorce, young sir' [414], and the dream of love collides with the political and social reality which will not countenance it.

It has often been suggested that Polixenes' outburst forms a parallel to Leontes' destructive jealousy in the first movement of the play, and that both shatter a preceding pastoral harmony (for the equivalent harmony in I ii, *see above*, p. 16). However, Polixenes' rage has more specific motivation than Leontes'. It is to do with social status and succession to the throne – an issue more urgent, perhaps, to a Jacobean than to a modern audience, but readily understood by both as involving a conflict between the ideal world of romance and the real one of politics. The violence of Polixenes' language may be taken as evidence of irrational rather than rational forces at work; this is particularly true of his savage threat to Perdita, 'I'll have thy beauty scratched with briers and made / More homely than thy state' [IV iv 422–3], and he is certainly behaving inconsistently with his previous argument in favour of grafting on the basis that

> we marry
> The gentler scion to the wildest stock,
> And make conceive a bark of baser kind
> By bud of nobler race.   [92–5]

Nevertheless, the impossibility of the union, granted that Perdita is what she appears to be, is a political reality that Perdita herself is quick to recognise: she must wake from her 'dream' and 'queen it no inch farther' [455–6]. The complicating element is that the audience know her to be in fact the daughter of a king; consequently they find a benevolent irony in the language of royalty which is applied to her. The romantic 'dream' is therefore not destroyed, but sustained by the totality of the situation in which the more immediate drama of her disqualification for marriage with Florizel takes place. The latter's continuing loyalty to romantic values – 'sorry, not afeard; delayed, / But nothing altered' [460–1] – is thus redeemed from appearing impossibly idealistic. Above all, his absolute 'faith' (asserted in the most uncompromising terms in lines 173–8), which appeals to transcendent values that seem to make a virtue of irrationality, stands in striking contrast to the irrational anger based on rational grounds just displayed by his father. Camillo, on the political level, urges him to 'Be advised', and Florizel, in a language of paradox that is to become increasingly important as the contradictions of 'high' and 'low' status are worked out in the action of the play, retorts,

> I am, and by my fancy. If my reason
> Will thereto be obedient, I have reason;
> If not, my senses, better pleased with madness,
> Do bid it welcome. [479–82]

This has the confidence and energy of youth, and as such is very much 'in character' for Florizel; it wins the approval of the audience, as it wins Camillo's, even while he pronounces it 'desperate' [482]. The audience, however, can see in it something more than the enthusiasm of youth. Without such romantic loyalty the drama cannot have a happy ending. Commitment that may look like 'madness' is to be preferred to more realistically rational behaviour; and this is accepted by the audience as a superior form of rationality, rather than something sub-rational, because of their awareness that Perdita justifies such commitment on both 'low' and 'high' grounds. They may not know the full terms in which a dénouement is to be effected, but they know enough to appreciate that worldly wisdom provides inadequate content for the 'reason' that this play now demands. The 'spring' movement thus progresses from a complex of refined and coarse pastoral, through melodramatic 'tragedy', to affirmation of an idealised and transcendent rationality which is sensed, if not yet properly understood, as containing the answer to the 'tragedy'.

The rounding-off of the scene is subordinated to this mood. It has the air of stage intrigue, but contrived in such a way as to suggest the work of a benevolently designing hand. The past and the future, as in the earlier speech of Time, are adroitly woven together. Thus Camillo's outline of his plan for Florizel and Perdita to present themselves at Leontes' court picks up again the 'winter' theme of Leontes' penitence, and the 'autumnal' mood of Act v is anticipated through the lines describing the welcome that Camillo imagines will await the young people in Sicilia [544–51]. His intention to reveal their escape to Polixenes, which sounds like a betrayal of their 'faith' (though the audience may give him credit for expecting a happier outcome) is balanced by Autolycus's decision not to do anything of the kind: 'If I thought it were a piece of honesty to acquaint the King withal, I would not do't. I hold it the more knavery to conceal it; and therein am I constant to my profession' [675–8]. On the other hand, Autolycus is prepared to deceive the Shepherd and his son into thinking that he will plead their case to Polixenes when he intends to curry favour by bringing them to Florizel. Such examples of deviousness, for good or bad motives, suggest the contrivances and schemings which necessarily form the material of human plots, while giving the audience a dim sense that something other than what human beings consciously intend is afoot. The comedy of Autolycus's playing on his victims' fears is especially appropriate here. His very exaggeration converts terror into laughter; and the innocent ignorance of the rustics, counterpointed against his knowing baseness, plays a further variation on Nature v. Art, Country v. Court, in which the complacent superiority apparently enjoyed by wit becomes an ambiguous advantage. There is, in fact, an undertow to events confirming the 'reason' of Florizel against the rationality of the schemers, and giving the contrivances of plot another dimension.

7   AUTUMN: THE CHANGED LEONTES

With the opening of v i, the first scene of the 'autumn' movement, there is another change of mood:

> Sir, you have done enough, and have performed
> A saint-like sorrow. No fault could you make
> Which you have not redeemed; indeed, paid down
> More penitence than done trespass.   [1–4]

There is a deep mellowing of tone and atmosphere. The image now presented of Leontes is that not only of an older man, but of one who has absorbed a radically transforming experience. Awareness of guilt has penetrated his very being, and with it has come knowledge of the devastating effect of his conduct towards Hermione. At his elbow, as almost a physical embodiment of his conscience, is the figure of Paulina, insistently reminding him of the incomparable virtues of the Queen whom he 'killed' (repeated three times, lines 15–17).

It is also Paulina who recapitulates the condition laid down by the oracle in the 'winter' movement of the play that the King shall have no heir till his lost child is found, and who emphasises the impossibility of this happening within the terms conceivable to ordinary rationality:

> Which that it shall
> Is all as monstrous to our human reason
> As my Antigonus to break his grave
> And come again to me . . . .   [40–3]

Such words, however, hint at another level of being, even while they seem to reject it; and the way Paulina speaks of the possibility of Leontes' remarrying is similarly ambivalent. She insists that he may only do so with her 'free leave', which will be given only when his 'first queen's again in breath; / Never till then' [83–4]. Since both Leontes and the audience are fully persuaded that Hermione is dead, this seems a purely rhetorical emphasis on her uniqueness, intended to prevent Leontes' being diverted away from his penitent focus on his lost Queen to the political concern for an heir which his courtiers are urging upon him. But the negative formulation does, of course, have its effect – chiefly in adjusting the minds of the audience to the seemingly impossible as being at least a remote possibility, and in preparing Leontes for a thawing of his frozen condition of remorse without lessening the tender awareness of Hermione which seems inseparable from it.

With the news of Florizel's, and in particular Perdita's, approach this delicate balance is apparently disturbed. The Gentleman who brings the report (a court poet, it would seem) is so transported by his enthusiasm that he forgets, till Paulina reminds him, the praise he had earlier bestowed on Hermione; and on actually seeing his unknown daughter Leontes reacts to her almost as a lover. The rational explanation for this is to be found in the close resemblance between parents and children. Florizel is so true a copy of his father, Polixenes, that Leontes is reminded of their youthful friendship; and, though, naturally enough, no comparable comment is made on Perdita, the sight of her and her would-be husband stirs Leontes to thoughts of his own lost children, with the Perdita–Hermione connection, therefore, not far beneath the surface. These lines of continuity merge with the religious motifs in the language to make Florizel and Perdita a 'gracious couple' whose arrival evokes from the King the significant cry, 'Welcome hither / As is the spring to th'earth!' [150–1]. Lines 167–77 also associate them with a prayer that the 'blessed gods' should 'Purge all infection from our air'; and the exalted language ('holy', 'graceful', 'sacred') which he applies to the absent Polixenes further defines Leontes' changed state of mind. His sense of sin makes him acutely aware of his 'issueless' condition, but it also prompts him to greater sympathy with the creatures who stand before him as examples of what his own offspring might have been:

> What might I have been,
> Might I a son and daughter now have looked on,
> Such goodly things as you!   [175–7]

The reverse to this which the reported arrival of Polixenes seems to bring about is only temporary. Florizel and Perdita have won Leontes as a friend through their own innate virtues, which strike the deepest chord of response from him at this particular moment and in this particular mood; hence the containment of yet another threat of destruction is assured.

8 AUTUMN: REVELATIONS

The revelations for which v i has created the necessary atmosphere occur in two stages, and in two dramatically different modes. The first, in v ii, is presented indirectly, with a switch from verse to prose, and from action to narration, which serves the obvious purpose of lowering the tension so that the climactic dénouement can be reserved for the final scene and the bringing of Hermione's statue to life. Nevertheless, this is by no means a low-key scene. The 'wonder' already aroused by the appearance of Florizel and Perdita at the Sicilian court in the previous scene is again the reiterated burden of the Gentlemen who report the discovery of Perdita's identity in 'very notes of admiration', and an ineffable extravagance of feeling is both the theme and style of their speeches. They are self-consciously sophisticated courtiers, given to expressing themselves in slightly bizarre images that recall the 'wit' of Metaphysical poetry – for instance, 'One of the prettiest touches of all, and that which angled for mine eyes – caught the water though not the fish' [80–2]; and yet through their courtly fantasticalness shines a primitive 'extremity' of emotion that recalls the emphasis on folk tale in the play's title and Mamillius's scene with his mother (*see above*, p. 10). Astonishment is such that 'ballad-makers cannot be able to express it' [24–5], the news is 'so like an old tale that the verity of it is in strong suspicion' [28–9], and the death of Antigonus is 'Like an old tale still, which will have matter to rehearse, though credit be asleep . . .' [59–60]. Moreover, extremes meet in a tragi-comic collision of joy wading in tears, with Leontes 'ready to leap out of himself for joy of his found daughter', and then, 'as if that joy were now become a loss', crying out, 'O, thy mother, thy mother' [48–50]. This is not simply satire on courtly affectation. The reunion is shown as if through a verbal screen which decoratively distorts, yet paradoxically enhances, the compulsive power of what is reported. The world of the Court becomes a world quivering and transported by elemental passions which shake it out of its artificial composure; the new life galvanises the old, and its reverberations are felt throughout the whole theatre.

The second half of v ii is something like a burlesque
anti-masque to this courtly extravaganza; but it is continuous
with, rather than antithetical to, what goes before. Here
Autolycus, the ex-courtier who has patronised the rustics, is
forced now to humour his promoted gulls. The paradox of
primitive emotion in sophisticated guise, which is the hallmark
of the first part of the scene, is parodied in the luxurious clothes
which turn the Clown into 'a gentleman born'; and the
marvelling over close family ties which have been rediscovered
and renewed, is travestied in the royal kinship which he can
now boast of: 'for the King's son took me by the hand, and
called me brother; and then the two kings called my father
brother; and then the Prince my brother and the Princess my
sister called my father father' [136–9]. Autolycus's promise to
amend his life is likewise a parody of Leontes' repentance;
though, as Schanzer observes, the word-play on being 'a tall
fellow of thy hands' at lines 158–67 is ambiguous (it can refer to
either bravery or picking of pockets): 'We are clearly not meant
to think of Autolycus as in any way reformed at the end of the
play' (New Penguin edn, p. 231). The audience know that he
will go on being a thief, but the euphoria of the Shepherd and
the Clown (particularly excited in the Shepherd by his naïve
equation of gentility with gentleness: 'for we must be gentle,
now we are gentlemen' [148–9]) covers his unregenerate
nature. His courtly self becomes dependent on that innate
goodness of the rustics which originally enabled him to dupe
them; and the whole scene ends with the Clown's new-found
status ironically, yet delightfully, being asserted to give protec-
tion to Autolycus's unregenerate character.

The second, and supreme, revelation comes in v iii. The shift
is now to direct presentation, with the miraculous moment of
the statue's being brought to life as its climax. The very fact
that this is an ensemble scene, with almost the entire cast on the
stage, is itself a signal that the plot is nearing culmination; and
the polite, but slightly comic, exchange of courtesies between
Leontes and Paulina as she displays the 'many singularities' of
her gallery only emphasises that the true emotional centre of
attention is the image of Hermione which all have been
assembled to see. This is kept, says Paulina, 'Lonely, apart' –
an implicit stage direction which leads most editors to suppose

that it stands in some curtained recess (though the Folio text reads, 'Louely, apart', which might mean simply 'with loving care'); and its revelation is preluded with words which raise the emotional temperature still higher:

> But here it is: prepare
> To see the life as lively mocked as ever
> Still sleep mocked death.   [18–20]

Ambiguities are carefully packed up in these words: 'mocked' means 'imitated', but carries the overtone of 'parody'; 'lively' plays on 'life', with the primary sense of 'verisimilitude', but a secondary sense of 'living mockery of life'; and 'sleep', though it 'mocks' death by seeming indistinguishable from it, also hints at a suspension of life which is restorative rather than mortal. It may be argued that such subtleties are afterthoughts derived from leisurely study of the text – that in the theatre these words can only be a comment on the realism of the statue. Hints have already been conveyed, however, in v i that the impossibility of Hermione's being again the wife of Leontes, though 'monstrous' to human reason, might exist as some curious kind of possibility; and the verbal play in Paulina's words serves to keep this paradox, if only subliminally, in being. At the very least, she is an exhibitor with an astonishing exhibit to display, which she proceeds to make the most of, as she works up her audience's expectations, and at last draws the curtain, exclaiming, 'Behold, and say 'tis well!' [v iii 20].

When this has been done, Paulina speaks words that again seem to convey an implicit stage direction: 'I like your silence: it the more shows off / Your wonder' [21–2]. In thus responding with awe-struck silence to the revelation of the statue the audience on the stage in effect guides the response of the audience in the actual theatre, making it one of astonishment at the spectacle of Art so closely imitating Nature. Nevertheless, the theatre audience's response is necessarily more complex than that of the stage audience. In the theatre the 'statue' has almost certainly to be represented by the actress (in the Jacobean theatre it would, of course, have been a boy) who earlier took the part of Hermione, and since the audience do not know that Hermione has been kept alive they are most likely to suppose that the same person is being used in order to suggest the marvellous realism of the statue (the work, they remember, of 'that rare Italian master, Julio Romano, who, had he himself eternity and could put breath into his work, would beguile Nature of her custom, so perfectly he is her ape' [v ii 95–8]). An imaginative dimension is added to this realism in that the audience are invited, via Leontes' surprise and Paulina's explanation, to note the aging-effect introduced by the artist to suggest that this is how Hermione would have looked after the passage of sixteen years. At the same time, however, the realism approximates to the theatrical reality as the living stage impersonator, though supposedly representing the coldness of stone, inevitably betrays signs of 'warm life', and the other characters on stage begin to react to the statue as if it were indeed alive – Perdita needing to be restrained from kissing its hand on the pretext that the colours are still wet, Paulina being afraid that Leontes' fancy will make him think it moves, and both kings thinking it actually breathes, the strangeness of which is beautifully caught in Leontes'

> Still methinks
> There is an air comes from her. What fine chisel
> Could ever yet cut breath?   [v iii 77–9]

By such means both stage and theatre audience are gradually advanced towards the acceptance of an art so natural that it seems capable of cancelling their rational distinctions between truth and imitation, and to a condition in which they share with Leontes the belief that 'No settled senses of the world can match / The pleasure of that madness' [72–3].

Such consummation is made dramatic reality in the final animation of the statue. By this time the paradox of the situation has been pushed almost to the brink of absurdity; it must not be prolonged much further if it is to avoid toppling over into anti-climax. Yet the only way forward is by the creation of an effect which is still more astonishing and in defiance of all normal standards of credibility. Accordingly, Paulina is given words which screw the already heightened tension a notch higher, while also promising release:

> Either forbear,
> Quit presently the chapel, or resolve you
> For more amazement. If you can behold it,
> I'll make the statue move indeed, descend
> And take you by the hand . . . .   [85–9]

The possibility that this might be regarded as black magic is introduced only to banish what might otherwise be a barrier to the state of mind necessary for the virtual miracle that Paulina is about to perform; and the corollary is her final evocation of what is tantamount to a religious commitment: 'It is required / You do awake your faith' [94–5]. What follows is, appropriately, a kind of incantation, accompanied by music and punctuated with pauses which create a solemnly ritualistic tone unique in the verse of this play:

> 'Tis time: descend; be stone no more; approach;
> Strike all that look upon with marvel.   [99–100]

It is an intensely theatrical moment, yet also perfectly natural in effect. The repeated commands seem to coax limbs grown stiff with their frozen posture into unaccustomed movement, tacitly matching action to the symbolic hints of life overcoming death in 'I'll fill your grave up' and 'Bequeath to death your numbness, for from him / Dear life redeems you' [101–2].

The awakening of the statue is thus strongly impregnated with religious feeling; yet for the theatre audience, as opposed to the one on the stage, it is a piece of beautifully organised spectacle. And even for the stage audience it is, as Fitzroy Pyle remarks, 'shown to be consistent both with common sense and with a sense of miracle' (*'The Winter's Tale': A Commentary on the Structure*, p. 137). It is the ultimate reconciliation of Art and Nature, leading to the wonder of life restored, but returning those who share in it to an enhanced awareness of ordinary experience. Leontes is at first too awed and astonished to think of touching his rewon wife; but he is urged to do so in words that dissolve the forbidding strangeness with a properly humanising touch of humour [105–7], and when he does present his hand (the 'stage direction' is incorporated in the dialogue at line 107) his own words set the seal on the recovery of normality:

> O, she's warm!
> If this be magic, let it be an art
> Lawful as eating.   [109–11]

As the tension had been carefully wound up to the climactic animation of the statue, so it is wound down at the end to the happy ending required by the genre of comedy: Leontes embraces his wife; Perdita kneels to receive her mother's blessing; questions are asked which imply a rational explanation of these astonishing events (though the answers are not given, but wisely left to the imagination of the audience); and Paulina is snatched from her sentimental – and decidedly out-of-character – intention of withdrawing from society, and paired off by Leontes with Camillo. All who were 'dissevered' are rejoined; and, as Leontes leads his fellow-actors 'from hence' to enjoy their reunion at leisure, the audience take their cue to applaud and themselves leave the theatre. Having passed through the most shattering, as well as the most lyrically delightful and comically grotesque experiences, they are dismissed with the reassuring sense that the stability of time-honoured convention has been restored. The play has reached its autumnal fruition; and its 'tale' has been told.

PART TWO: PERFORMANCE

9 INTRODUCTION

In this section attention will be concentrated on the following four recent productions of *The Winter's Tale*:

1. The RSC production of 1969 at Stratford-upon-Avon, directed by Trevor Nunn; designed by Christopher Morley; music by Guy Woolfenden; Richard Pasco as Polixenes; Barrie Ingham as Leontes; Judi Dench as Hermione and Perdita; Brenda Bruce as Paulina; Derek Smith as Autolycus.
2. The RSC production of 1976 at Stratford-upon-Avon, directed by John Barton and Trevor Nunn; designed by Di Seymour; music by Guy Woolfenden; Ian McKellen as Leontes; John Woodvine as Polixenes; Marilyn Taylerson as Hermione; Cherie Lunghi as Perdita; Barbara Leigh-Hunt as Paulina; Michael Williams as Autolycus.
3. The BBC television production of 1980, directed by Jane Howell; designed by Don Homfray; music by Dudley Simpson; Jeremy Kemp as Leontes; Robert Stephens as Polixenes; Anna Calder-Marshall as Hermione; Debbie Farrington as Perdita; Margaret Tyzack as Paulina; Rikki Fulton as Autolycus.
4. The RSC production of 1981 at Stratford-upon-Avon (Barbican, 1982), directed by Ronald Eyre; designed by Chris Dyer; music by Stephen Oliver; Patrick Stewart as Leontes; Ray Jewers as Polixenes; Gemma Jones as Hermione; Julia Hills as Perdita; Sheila Hancock as Paulina; Geoffrey Hutchings as Autolycus.

Other productions, notably in Canada and the USA, have made significant contributions to the theatrical interpretation of *The Winter's Tale*, but I have preferred to deal with productions that I have myself seen, and some, if not all, of which are likely to have been seen by a fair proportion of readers. As will be inferred from the comments I make, my own opinion of the success of these four productions varies considerably from one to another. Each one, however, incorporates a distinctive approach to the play and its problems. That none is ideal matters less than that none is without fruitful insights, or, it may be, examples of interesting experiment, even if they did not come off. I also prefer not to review each production individually, but to focus on aspects of the play which can be variously illuminated by these different productions – my aim being less to tell about productions than to allow productions to tell about the dramatic possibilities inherent in the play.

From its first recorded production on 15 May 1611 *The Winter's Tale* has fluctuated both in popularity and critical esteem. Most seventeenth-century references are to performances at Court, but the frequently quoted 1611 reference is to a production by the King's Men at the Globe Theatre recorded by Simon Forman in his *Booke of Plaies*. His summary of the plot concentrates on Leontes' jealousy, the oracle and the discovery of Perdita's true identity. There is no mention of the statue's coming to life; it is the Autolycus scenes which seem to have made the most impact on Forman:

> Remember also the Rog that cam in all tottered like coll pixci / and howe he feynd him sicke & to haue bin Robbed of all that he had and howe he cosoned the por man of all his money. and after cam to the shep sher with a pedlers packe & there cosened them Again of all their money. And howe he changed apparrell wt the Kinge of bomia his sonn. and then howe he turned Courtiar &c / beware of trustinge feined beggars or fawninge fellouse.
>
> (Variorum edn, pp. 318–19)

This does not necessarily indicate that all the focus of attention was on Autolycus and the earlier part of the play. When it was performed at Court contemporary interest in the masque is likely to have given the statue scene special prominence; and in this connection Dennis Bartholomeusz, who has written the most comprehensive stage history of *The Winter's Tale*, suggests that, although Shakespeare's dances in IV iv were probably influenced by Court fashion, his statue scene was such an original success that it was in its turn an influence on Court writers such as Thomas Campion, particularly in *The Lord's Masque* (*'The Winter's Tale' in Performance*, p. 27).

In the eighteenth century, which revived *The Winter's Tale* after a century's neglect, neo-classical critical standards operated against the 'wide gap of time' in the play's structure, and sentimental interest favoured the story of the young lovers rather than the jealousy of Leontes. The result was a staging of versions which omitted the first three acts and focused on the sheep-shearing festival in Act IV and the revelations of Act V. In the most successful of these, David Garrick's version, aptly entitled *Florizel and Perdita, A Dramatic Pastoral* (Drury Lane Theatre, 1756), the setting is Bohemia throughout; the business of Acts I–III is narrated to the audience in a specially written dialogue between Camillo and a conveniently ignorant Gentleman; and Leontes is brought to Polixenes' shores by the storm which in Shakespeare's original accompanied Antigonus's exposure of the infant Perdita. Garrick himself played Leontes, and, according to his biographer, Thomas Davies, 'his action and whole behaviour, during the supposed disenchanting of Hermione, was extremely affecting' (*Memoirs of the Life of David Garrick* [1780], quoted in the Arden edn, p. 177). The emphasis on sentiment is made evident both in the speeches which in this version are written into the text, and in its stage directions. For example, in place of v iii 109–11 (*see above*, p. 44) Garrick has the following more emotionally expansive lines:

> Support me, Gods!
> If this be more than visionary bliss
> My reason cannot hold; my wife! my queen!
> But speak to me, and turn me wild with transport,
> I cannot hold me longer from these arms;
> She's warm! she lives!

And not only is there an embrace between Hermione and Leontes (as in Shakespeare), but also a doubling-up of effect with an exclamation from Perdita of 'O *Florizel*!' and a stage direction which reads: '*Perdita* leans on *Florizel*'s bosom' (Variorum edn, p. 411).

In the nineteenth century such famous names as Kemble, Macready and Charles Kean played the part of Leontes, and actresses equally famous, such as Mrs Siddons and Helen

Faucit, took the role of Hermione. The most celebrated performance, however, was that directed by Charles Kean (Princess Theatre, 1856), which made its effect through lavishness of production rather than excellence of acting. Both the tragic and comic halves of the play were retained (though with many drastic cuts), but the emphasis was shifted to scenic spectacle and a curiously misconceived archaeological realism. As Bartholomeusz remarks, 'We have an early example here of the habit still common among producers of imposing an interpretation on Shakespeare's text which has no connection with its essential deeper life, but is attractive enough to fascinate an audience' (p. 82). Kean followed Thomas Hanmer, who in his edition of the play (in 1744) had substituted Bithynia for Shakespeare's Bohemia (thus overcoming the pedantic objection that Bohemia has no seacoast), and on this slight hint elaborate costumes and carefully researched decor were created in order to suggest the contrast between a classically Greek Sicilia and a more romantically Asiatic Bohemia/Bythinia (with associations with Troy and the Trojans). 'I have endeavoured,' claimed Kean in the note which he printed along with the announcement of his production,

> and I hope not altogether in vain, by the united accessories of painting, music, and architecture, in conjunction with the rapid movements and multiplied life which belong to the stage alone, to re-embody the past; trusting that the combination may be considered less an exhibition of pageantry appealing to the eye, than illustration of history addressed to the understanding.

Whatever its educational value as history, there is no doubt about the sensational appeal which this production made to both eye and ear. The enthusiasm of contemporary audiences is caught by J. W. Cole in his *Life and Theatrical Times of Charles Kean* (1859) as he describes the impact of this version's opening:

> As the curtain rose, we saw before us Syracuse at the epoch of her highest prosperity, about 330 B.C., and gazed on the fountains of Arethusa and the temple of Minerva. After the short introductory scene between *Camillo* and *Archidamus*, we passed to the banqueting-hall in the Royal palace, where *Leontes, Polixenes, Hermione*, and guests were discovered reclining on couches, after the

1. Trevor Nunn's RSC production, Stratford, 1969, I ii. Judi Dench as Hermione, Jeremy Richardson as Mamillius, Barrie Ingham as Leontes (on rocking horse with Mamillius) and Richard Pasco as Polixenes. This 'nursery' setting emphasises the innocent playfulness of the opening, as well as providing psychological implications which can be developed later in the production. Photograph © Joe Cocks.

2. Trevor Nunn's RSC production, Stratford, 1969, II iii. Brenda Bruce as Paulina (holding the infant Perdita) and Barrie Ingham as Leontes. The chessboard motif emphasises Leontes' abstraction from normal humanity (in contrast to the courtiers' natural interest in the new baby). The colours of the pieces are white and red, echoing the white of Leontes and Sicilia *vs* the red of Polixenes and Bohemia. Photograph © Joe Cocks.

3. Ronald Eyre's RSC production, Stratford, 1981, and Barbican, 1982, IV i.
Robert Eddison as Time. Time also appears as the centre-piece of the
opening pageant in this production. Photograph © Joe Cocks.

4. Jane Howell's BBC television production, 1980, IV iii. Ricki Fulton as Autolycus stealing the purse of the Clown (Paul Jesson). The theft is made both plausible and amusing by the Clown's close embrace as he lifts up the supposedly wounded Autolycus. Photograph © BBC copyright.

5. Ronald Eyre's RSC production, Stratford, 1981, and Barbican, 1982, IV iv. Geoffrey Hutchings as Autolycus (in top hat and flamboyant bow-tie), singing a ballad with Susan Jane as Mopsa and Clare Travers-Deacon as Dorcas. The Victorian rusticity of the other characters in this scene indicates the jollified pastiche quality of Eyre's treatment of the sheep-shearing festival. Photograph © Joe Cocks.

6. John Barton and Trevor Nunn's RSC production, Stratford, 1976, V iii. Marilyn Taylerson as Hermione (on pedestal as the 'statue' about to come to life), Barbara Leigh-Hunt as Paulina, Ian McKellen as Leontes and, on either side of him, Cherie Lunghi as Perdita and Nicholas Grace as Florizel. Photograph © Joe Cocks.

manner of the ancient Greeks. Musicians were playing the hymn to *Apollo*, and slaves supplied wine and garlands. Thirty-six resplendently handsome young girls, representing youths in complete warlike panoply, entered, and performed the evolutions of the far-famed Pyrrhic dance. The effect was electrical, and established at the commencement an impression of what might be expected as the play advanced.   (pp. 169–70)

Equally elaborate (and irrelevant) reconstructions followed in the later scenes of the play. The trial of Hermione took place in the Theatre at Syracuse, with the stage, again in Cole's words, presenting 'an astonishing instance of scenic illusion . . . by pictorial and mechanical combination, it appeared to expand to the colossal proportions which we read of as belonging to the most celebrated of those ancient buildings in which thirty thousand persons might be seated on the benches.' But perhaps the most 'original' effect, which probably remained in many spectators' minds as the *pièce de résistance* of the evening, was Kean's device for improving on Shakespeare's means of bridging the time interval between Acts III and IV:

Clouds now descended and filled the stage, leading to a classical allegory, representing the course of *Time*. As these clouds dispersed, *Selene*, or *Luna*, was discovered in her car, accompanied by the *Stars*, (personified by living figures), and gradually sunk into the ocean. *Time* then appeared, surmounting the globe, no longer represented by the traditionary bald-headed elder, with his scythe and hour-glass, but as a classical figure, more in accordance with the character of the play as now represented. He spoke the lines with which Shakespeare has connected the two separate epochs of his play.   (p. 172)

The mere words were eclipsed by an equally stupendous *tableau vivant* of *Phoebus* rising 'with surpassing brilliancy in the chariot of the Sun', borrowed from Flaxman's engraving of the 'Shield of Achilles'. The 'entire allegory', raved Cole, 'may be pronounced the greatest triumph of art ever exhibited on the stage'.

The reaction against such subordination of words to spectacle came at the beginning of the twentieth century in the experimental productions of Harley Granville-Barker at the

Savoy Theatre, and it was with *The Winter's Tale* (1912) that he began his revolutionary style. As is often the case with 'newness' in the arts, innovation meant going back to the source of things. Without attempting to re-create the exact conditions of Shakespeare's own theatre Granville-Barker sought to adapt the modern proscenium-arch stage to the fluidity and freedom, and the primacy of verbal-*cum*-imaginative appeal, which characterised the apron stage of the Elizabethan and Jacobean theatre. By building a platform over the orchestra pit, from which an actor could speak with plausible intimacy direct to the audience, Barker immediately transformed the Shakespearean soliloquy into an acceptable convention, and by replacing the footlights with overhead illumination he reduced dependence on elaborate lighting-plans. Above all, he eliminated both the imaginatively inhibiting effect of realistic scenery and its deplorable slowing-down of the play's action (because of the need to strike scenes) by opting for a much simpler and more stylised set painted in white and gold. These conditions, making for greater speed of performance, also enabled him to present Shakespeare's text in a version much less drastically cut than had become the established practice; and, though he added elements of extravagance of his own, particularly in the costumes designed by Albert Rothenstein, supposedly in the manner of 'that rare Italian master, Julio Romano' (on the strength of v ii 95), these were planned, as J. L. Styan remarks, 'for the release of the imagination into the world of artifice' (*The Shakespeare Revolution* [Cambridge, 1977] p. 87). The result, at any rate for the contemporary critic, John Palmer, was 'probably the first performance in England of a play by Shakespeare that the author would have recognized for his own since Burbage' (*Saturday Review*, 28 Sep 1912, quoted in Bartholomeusz, p. 162). It was not, however, anything like an exercise in historical reconstruction. Essentially, this was just as much a modern production as its predecessors, reinterpreting Shakespeare in a style recognisably early-twentieth-century; by being more faithful to Shakespeare it contrived to be truer to the spirit of its own time. Unfortunately, this did not make it a popular production; and, although it was an artistic success, being praised and appreciated for its significantly innovatory qualities by several discerning reviewers and theatre-goers, it was a box-office failure and had to be taken off after only six weeks. Nevertheless, the influence of this, and other subsequent Granville-Barker productions of Shakespeare, was immense, and is still detectable in the work of present-day directors. It put an end once and for all to the overblown spectacle of nineteenth-century productions in which scenery tyrannised over the text, and it restored Shakespearean dramaturgy to something like its own.

10   SETS AND COSTUMES

In the view of Stephen Wall *The Winter's Tale* is an especially difficult play to produce. It belongs to the genre of 'romance', and this, he suggests, was enough to bind its component elements together for its original audience (though how this assumption worked is not clear); but the problem today is how to find 'a production style which faithfully conveys the purposefulness of the story's mythic undertow, but which also allows full expression of the eddying contingencies of its episodes' (*TLS*, 10 July 1981). This comment occurs in a review of the 1981 Stratford production, and forms part of a discussion of the style evolved by Ronald Eyre to meet the problems posed by the play's fusion of diverse romance material, and, in particular, the choice of a tall, spare, almost austere, set, which demands that the audience fill it with their own imaginative realisation of the words they hear. Mr Wall was quite unconvinced by this solution: 'The high and blank-walled permanent set', he wrote dismissively, 'suggests some loading-bay abandoned by the National Theatre.'

On the other hand, Roger Warren, reviewing the same director's work, approved of what he saw as 'a chamber production', which provided 'an apt setting' for the unusually light, flippant interpretation of Leontes' jealousy offered by the actor Patrick Stewart (*Shakespeare Survey 35*, 1981). One man's meat is, of course, another man's poison, but such differences of response by two intelligent reviewers indicate more than that.

Mr Wall is right in suggesting that the modern director cannot rely on the existence of a ready-made convention which is accepted by the audience, and within which he can unfold the variations and contradictions of *The Winter's Tale* with the confidence that they will find their own natural place. He has to make the very style of his production the means by which he creates an appropriate convention. Directing becomes, in fact, a deliberate matter of adopting a certain reading of the play and finding theatrical images to interpret that reading to the audience. What the different comments of the critics are thus likely to reveal are differences of opinion about the interpretation of the play, and different judgements on the success with which interpretation has been embodied in forms that effectively, and convincingly, project it in the theatre.

Sets and costumes are among the most obvious means by which interpretation can be expressed. They are the first things the audience become aware of, and they powerfully, sometimes overpoweringly, communicate atmosphere. The design created by Chris Dyer for Eyre's 1981 production consisted of a square area at the centre of the stage covered by a cloth, which three young men ceremoniously folded up to mark the start of the performance. The costumes to be donned by the actors were displayed on tailor's dummies, which remained visible to the audience throughout the play. To Gareth Lloyd Evans this was a contemptible device, 'a clapped-out visual cliché unworthy of the RSC', which he regarded as an entirely superfluous way of signalling that this was to be 'a non-naturalistic lark' (*Stratford-upon-Avon Herald*, 10 July 1981). After the prelude of I i the true action began with a courtly dance, followed by the opening of the double doors in the blank wall at the back to astonish the audience with a Twelfth Night Pageant of Time, awesomely grotesque and completely dominating the stage. At the hour of midnight (denoted by the courtiers counting up to twelve) Time seemed to part his own loins to reveal a playful Mamillius. In her interesting discussion of the production (in 'Emblematic Figures in *The Winter's Tale*') Kathleen Gledhill takes this to mean that 'Mamillius represents Truth, hidden by Time until at the appropriate time, Time turns from Concealer to Revealer' (p. 17); and such a view, it must be admitted, is amply supported by the programme notes which accompanied

Eyre's production. These supplied information, and attractive illustrations, from Jacobean pictorial representations of Time, together with liberal amounts of quotation from various critics (but especially Professor Inga-Stina Ewbank) and passages from *Pandosto* – including the lengthy explanatory extension of its title emphasising the theme of 'the Triumph of Time': 'Wherein is discovered by a pleasant Historie, that although by the means of sinister fortune, Truth may be concealed yet by Time in spight of fortune it is most manifestly revealed.' For the audience, however, such an allegorical interpretation tended to remain at the level of literary commentary. The pageant of Time undoubtedly made a very striking impact, and the creation of a carnival atmosphere in which something grotesque gave birth to new life may perhaps have suggested the essentially tragi-comic nature of what was to follow; but it was the arbitrariness of the event which made the strongest impression. It did not seem that Time was directing and controlling the action, but rather that a bizarre 'happening' was taking place – the strange figure unaccountably burst into the empty space, filled it with its own fantastic life, and then disappeared again. The effect was, if anything, to underline the artificiality of the theatrical experience already suggested by the tailor's dummies, and further counter any expectations of realism that the audience might have entertained.

The double doors through which Time entered also opened later in the production to admit the procession bringing Apollo's oracle to the trial scene; and it was through them that the outlandishly huge bear that kills Antigonus was glimpsed in terrifying flashes of lightning, that Time made its entry as Chorus in iv i, and that the statue of Hermione was revealed in the final scene. All these were modes of imprinting an image on the empty stage; and thus, if symbolic, symbolic of the actual process by which the action before them was imprinting its image on the mind of the audience.

In the 1969 production directed by Trevor Nunn – probably the most famous (or notorious) of the four productions under discussion – the opening set was of a very different kind. With a reminiscence of Granville-Barker, the stage was white, but there was nothing derivative about the way the performance actually began. The stage was plunged in darkness, broken only by garish flashes of light which revealed Leonardo da Vinci's Renaissance man 'changed to a helpless figure spinning in a transparent box: a heroic emblem transformed to that of time's fool' (Irving Wardle, *The Times*, 16 May 1969). Words were spoken from the opening of Time's speech in IV i, in a slow, portentous manner, and with a strange negro accent (when the full speech came in its due place, i.e. just before the sheep-shearing festival, it was contrastingly spoken in a lighter and brisker manner). Then to the chiming of a music box an all-white Leontes appeared on the white rocking-horse of his son, Mamillius, the setting now being seen as a stylised nursery with white boxes and toys, some of which, notably a humming-top that gave out an eerie, resonant hum, became properties in the subsequent action. The emphasis was thus laid on playfulness and the exchange of 'innocence for innocence', but against a sinister prologue which mysteriously suggested the possibility of tragic alteration. The effect of the music box in particular was to give greater prominence to the connection of the nursery setting with harmony and innocence, and it was heard again, with pathetic or ironic overtones, at subsequent moments in the play (for example, between I ii and II i; between II ii and II iii – though not between III i and III ii; as a prelude, giving way to sea sounds, before the move to Bohemia in III iii; and, with especially poignant echoes, between V i and V ii).

The merit of this set was that it gave a stimulus to the audience's imagination, introducing motifs that could be repeated with telling variations later, and yet managed to avoid the embarrassing sense of what Granville-Barker deplored as the self-consciously 'poetical'. For some critics it was marred by what they saw as its heavy-handed Freudian symbolism – for them the nursery more than merely hinted that Leontes' jealousy was a psychotic condition, a complex which, like all complexes, had its roots in childhood. Given his avowed intention to present Shakespeare to contemporary audiences in a way that would have the immediacy of a contemporary reality, it may well be that Trevor Nunn intended an effect of this kind; but, if so, his set by no means pointed exclusively to such an interpretation. It was a brilliantly conceived, but essentially evocative and open-ended, visual metaphor, capitalising on the childhood images already there in Shakespeare's text, and heightening awareness of them rather than limiting them to one fashionable twentieth-century meaning.

 A quite different set – though it was, again, one of a stylised nature – was used in Trevor Nunn's collaboration with John Barton in their 1976 production. The keynote was Scandinavian, and much use was made of Eskimo-like dress; of runic symbols on rugs and curtains and on fabrics which were stretched over wooden-framed chairs; and, above all, of the motif of the bear. Through this seemingly perverse transfer from the Mediterranean world nominally adopted by Shakespeare (or the real English world that shows through it at several points) to an arctic world for which the text offers no excuse, the directors sought to bounce the audience into a more acute awareness of primitive levels of opposition between winter and summer. This was reinforced by an elaborately beautiful programme (becoming in this instance almost an essential part of the production) which explained the Scandinavian style in the following terms:

> The two solstice festivals were celebrated more intensely in Scandinavia than anywhere in the South. The Winter Solstice was called Jul and it marked the darkest day of the year. . . . For the Norsemen Jul was essentially a family festival and places were even laid for the dead ancestors . . . .

This was printed on a white double page with dark motifs, using dark-brown or orange type. Turning over, the next double page was a brilliantly warm orange, with the dark-brown motifs and print now seeming to glow intensely, and with an appropriate emphasis on the Summer Solstice as 'the most joyous celebration of the Nordic year . . . dedicated to the young, to dancing, garlands, light and new growth'.

 In the terms employed by such a production the structure of the play inevitably appeared as two- rather than three-part, and this was echoed in the use of symbols common to both halves. Thus the strange 'hieroglyphic' motifs which figured on the backcloth were shown as white on a dark background in Part One, and as black on a lighter, warmer brown in Part Two. The bear provided a thematic link between both parts: introduced in the form of a game in which Mamillius, armed with a toy harpoon, chased Polixenes, who covered himself with a rug to symbolise the bear, it curiously, but impressively, conducted Antigonus to his death in iii iii, and reappeared to remove its own head and deliver Time's bridging speech in iv i. Moreover, the curtains which initially surrounded the stage (they were later drawn back) provided an outline of the story in terms that might have been represented by primitive cave paintings, or a child's scrawls on a blackboard – ranging from stylised husband and wife figures, bodies in tombs, and a shipwreck; through a picture of a primitive feast and a female figure suggestive of Hermione; to a final picture of reconciliation and reunion, with tall figures for the older generation and smaller ones for the younger. The 'old tale' element was thus brought so much to the fore that it risked becoming a parody of itself; but, in spite of this defect, the set was successful in helping to create a dimension in which the audience could respond to the play as 'conventional' in a positive and untrivial sense.

As in so many other respects, the Jane Howell television version of 1980 was a reasonable compromise between the extremes of the three productions already discussed. Dom Homfray's design recalled both the whiteness of Nunn's (and Granville-Barker's) set and the Scandinavian emphasis of the Barton–Nunn production by its abstract, almost glacial, construction: two white conical towers were situated in front of two iceberg-like segments, between which the actors made their exits and entrances; and stage right of these stood a somewhat bleakly formalised tree, reminiscent of the tree which also formed part of the Barton–Nunn set (both also conveying a hint of the famous tree in Beckett's *Waiting for Godot*). In the trial scene the conical towers were removed, and in their stead iron railings appeared, and a red carpet was laid down, leading to a bold, red throne. In the sheep-shearing scene this colouring was changed to gold and green as the carpet was replaced with artificial grass, and lighting suffused everything in a warm, yellow glow; the tree likewise turned brown, and on it appeared some yellow foliage. Throughout, the set gave a strong sense of non-naturalistic reality, inhibiting the play's possibilities in the view of Stanley Wells: 'Nature is art; symbolism is enhanced; but the set's limitations . . . deny the romantic liberties of the tale' (*TLS*, 20 Feb 1981). This is a criticism, however, which does not take sufficiently into account the necessity for a television production to offset the built-in prejudices of the medium. The actors' style of delivery inevitably responds to the intimacy of the small screen with a realism beyond what even the most realistic theatre commands, and with such a play as *The Winter's Tale* there is a corresponding imperative to suggest, though not too blatantly, the artificiality of the form. This set might well have appeared too determinedly Cubist, but, as it was usually seen (to an extent that would not be the case in the theatre) as a background, glimpsed only in part beyond the shoulders of the cast, its abstract formality was not unduly emphasised.

Costumes for the Howell production were also modest. The dark fur worn by Leontes was slightly derivative from the Lapland costumes of Barton–Nunn, but no attempt was made to link him to a similar bear motif. The main effect was one of contrast with the white of Hermione and the lighter colour of Polixenes and Mamillius. The dressing of Leontes' own courtiers in a similar black suggested their subservience to him, though the subsequent action, in which Camillo rebels against the murderous role assigned him, and even the more conformist courtiers are horrified by their King's treatment of Hermione and her baby, made this seem a misleading emphasis. The most effective contrast was that created by the play's children. Mamillius appeared chasing a ball that rolled through the iceberg entrance, and he was the focus of the adults' affectionate attention. Likewise, a real baby Perdita acted as a compellingly vivid token of life and warmth, against the coldness of the set and the darkness of Leontes' dress.

11 LEONTES

The chief differences in the presentation of Leontes centred on the manner in which his jealousy arose. Barrie Ingham, in the 1969 Nunn production, enacted 'the demented breakdown of the schizophrenic' (Gordon Parso, *Morning Star*, 17 May 1969). Motivation and genesis were by-passed in a brilliant piece of directorial inventiveness which involved the use of stroboscopic lighting. The playful happiness of the nursery world was suddenly suspended as the light changed to a sinister, flickering blueness, conveying the subjective distortion created by Leontes' 'diseased opinion'. Passages such as his soliloquies at I ii 108–19 and 137–46 were thus isolated from the normal flow of action and thrillingly perceived by the audience as an eruptive violation of the state of innocence, with the stage action becoming essentially a psychological projection of Leontes' state of mind. This effect was further heightened by temporary freezing of the other players and, as at I ii 180–5, a change to miming which indicated the sexual intimacy imagined by Leontes as taking place between Polixenes and Hermione. Ingham also accentuated his lines so as to convey Leontes' distorted consciousness. In the soliloquy at I ii 185–207 he marked the bitterness of 'Inch-thick, knee-deep' with a cannon-ade of heavy stresses on each word, and he gave an unusual emphasis to both occurrences of the word 'this' in lines 192–3 ('And many a man there is even at *this* present, / Now, while I speak *this* . . .') to highlight his self-consciousness. Similarly, phrases such as 'No barricado for a belly' and 'bag and baggage' came out with an explosive force that turned the alliteration into tormented self-laceration. A little later, in his conversation with Camillo, the words 'Sicilia is a so-forth' – which Leontes now imagines to be on everyone's lips – were hissed in the sing-song delivery used by children when they mock each other, thus conveying both the childishness of his state of mind and its contrast with the true, and healthy, innocence of childhood.

Lighting-effects similar to those of 1969 were also used in the 1976 RSC production, and critics generally found that Ian McKellen's Leontes gave the impression of making a startling (though not always convincing) leap from healthy normality to contorted jealousy. According to Michael Billington, this Leontes conveyed 'a racked sexual anguish' by 'spitting out words like "sluiced" and "bedswerver"' (*Guardian*, 5 June 1976); and, in her Warwick thesis '*The Winter's Tale* in Production', Christine Wallwork describes him as having given the impression of being 'very repressed . . . given to nervous mannerisms, constantly smoothing his hair', his jealousy seemingly 'caused by a deep-rooted insecurity' (p. 33). Such attempts at psychological realism were, however, carefully subordinated to the production's overall concentration on myth. The jealousy retained the arbitrary 'once-upon-a-time' character of fairy tale; like Lear's division of his kingdom at the beginning of *King Lear*, it was something that had to be accepted so that the rest of the story could go on, rather than explained in terms of plausible motivation.

In the RSC production of 1981, however, Patrick Stewart gave a performance of Leontes which put all the emphasis on neurosis. His jealousy seemed inherent in the man from the very first, betraying itself in the manic enthusiasm of his initial distortion of playfulness into violent horseplay. His twisting of Polixenes' arm behind his back, as if to 'force' him into staying a little longer in Sicilia, and his roughly 'affectionate' treatment of Hermione, could be seen as evidence that he was already deeply disturbed by what the audience were subsequently to recognise as jealousy – in accordance with the critical view which sees Leontes as, in fact, jealous from before the play opens. The textual justification for this might be doubtful, but there was no denying the excellence of Patrick Stewart's performance – a brilliantly executed study in barely controlled hysteria.

In the BBC television version (1980) Jeremy Kemp delivered a more orthodox Leontes. Here also there were no stage tricks to indicate an abnormal consciousness; the camera's zooming-in to close-up was sufficient to mark his soliloquies, and the sense of contrast was gained by the simple, naturalistic device of having the father speak his suspicions direct to the viewer while holding his son, Mamillius, whose face was turned away. Full advantage was taken of the hints planted in Shakespeare's text: at I ii 87 ('At my request he would not') Leontes gave a slight look of surprise, a shadow of doubt, but no more, seeming to cross his mind, after which the dialogue continued normally. He started to look uneasy at the free chattering and embracing of Polixenes and Hermione; but even at lines 101–5 ('Three crabbèd months . . .') he was grave rather than embittered. At this point Leontes was in close-up with Hermione, then Polixenes joined with them to make a significant trio – Polixenes and the Queen appearing to be happily touched by this reference to wooing and final acceptance, while Leontes seemed moved, but also hurt, as if he now saw a meaning in the delay which he had not noticed before. This was the turning-point. With the soliloquy beginning at line 108, Polixenes and Hermione were left still chatting in a relaxed, unself-conscious manner, but Leontes remained in close-up, feeling his heart dance, 'But not for joy, not joy'. He was later (in II iii) a sick and weary man, but, as indicated by the text, this was presented as being a consequence of the self-torment and sleeplessness induced by his own jealousy. In all, Jeremy Kemp's Leontes was a tragic, rather than a deranged, figure, and to that extent one more capable of exciting pity than the other three.

The penitence of Leontes does not pose the same problems as his jealousy. The sense of a prolonged and far-reaching change is firmly created in the play's language, and the way is therefore adequately prepared for the sadder and wiser man who eventually reappears at the beginning of Act v. All four interpretations of the part did full justice to this essential transformation – though to have Leontes carried on to the stage as an afflicted and bed-ridden creature, as happened in Ronald Eyre's 1981 production, seemed a needlessly obvious overstatement of the point. (Its chief advantage was that it enabled the King to rise from his bed, at v i 150–1, as if inspired with new life by the 'spring' which the advent of Perdita and Florizel seems to bring from the countryside to the Court of Sicilia.) And, particularly in the three stage productions of 1969, 1976 and 1981, the subdued delivery adopted by each of the actors involved made its own eloquently effective contrast with the frenzy and ranting of the earlier, jealous Leontes. Likewise, the deference and respect which he showed to Paulina underlined the fact that his previously egotistical and self-enclosed assertiveness had given way to a willingness to heed the voice of unflattering truth.

12   HERMIONE AND PERDITA

In the 1969 RSC production Judi Dench played the parts of both Hermione and Perdita, as Mary Anderson had done at the

Lyceum in 1887. This involved the omission of the v iii 28–32 reference to the statue's appearing aged to suggest the passage of sixteen years; and likewise some ingenious movement by Judi Dench, who slipped off stage as Perdita – to be surreptiously replaced by a non-speaking actress of similar appearance – and, thanks to a manoeuvre for hiding the statue from Leontes' over-excited view, was able to take the place of the statue out of sight of the audience. It was impossible to do this without giving the audience some sense of what was happening, and their consciousness of the clever execution of the trick did, to that extent, detract from its emotional magic. However, the loss was compensated by certain gains. In particular, the relationship between, and symbolic identity of, mother and daughter were strikingly confirmed by their being visibly enacted by the same woman; and a further consequence was that Hermione seemed not to be absent throughout the whole of Act IV (as, indeed, she was not, since the same actress was there on the stage), but to live again in Perdita. This provided a structurally appropriate counterpart to the sense created in v i (*see* lines 123–9 and the comment above, p. 38) that Florizel is exactly his father, Polixenes', image. On the other hand, the doubling necessitated Judi Dench's playing the two roles in such deliberately differentiated styles that she was forced into the position of making a somewhat artificial display of her acting-skills. As with the statue trick, this tended to lead the audience's attention away from the immediate dramatic situation to admiration for Miss Dench's qualities as a star performer. By general consent she was better as Hermione than as Perdita – though Irving Wardle perhaps felt more strongly than most that 'Growing from exquisite playfulness to superb dignity as Leontes' wife, she [was] barely more than skittish as his daughter' (*The Times*, 16 May 1969). Her greatest moment was in III ii, when she fainted on hearing of Mamillius's death. The controlled movement, emphasised by a lighting-change to chilling blue, was superbly done, and made Paulina's 'look down / And see what death is doing' singularly appropriate.

The problem of differentiating the two parts did not arise with the three other productions, since in them they were not doubled. The manner in which Hermione was played in the earlier scenes was usually dictated by the director's strategy for presenting Leontes' jealousy (thus, whereas in the RSC 1981 production Gemma Jones's Hermione was swept along, and yet puzzled and disconcerted by the frenetic performance of Patrick Stewart, in the 1980 television version Anna Calder-Marshall was essentially a normal, happily relaxed woman till disturbed by evident signs of hostility from Leontes); but all came into their own in the trial scene, which they, rather than their husbands, tended to dominate, successfully communicating a sense of aristocratic self-control, coupled with a resentment, that still went along with devotion and love, at the injustice of the proceedings.

The various Perditas tended to be divided into those, such as Julia Hills (RSC 1981), who offered a decidedly rustic young woman whose speech and manners reflected the kind of upbringing she might actually have received from her foster-father, the Old Shepherd, and those, such as Cherie Lunghi (RSC 1976), who, according to Bartholomeusz, 'had no Warwickshire earthiness, not much sinless sensuality, but a quality of high, spiritual innocence' (p. 224) – an interpretation more in accord with the romantic genre of *The Winter's Tale*, and one which emphasised the difference between her and the Clown, Mopsa, Dorcas and co.

13   PAULINA

As in other respects which concerned acting style, Ronald Eyre's 1981 RSC production was responsible for the most controversial Paulina in the performance of Sheila Hancock. Roger Warren thoroughly approved of her interpretation: 'Most Paulinas are effective in a fearsomely humorous way; the immediately noticeable thing about this Paulina was that she was not fearsome at all, explaining patiently to the bureaucratic gaoler that the child is prisoner to the womb and now freed by nature.' In his view she delivered the melodramatic speech at III ii 173–200 (*see above*, p. 25) 'without a trace of rant but with maximum impact', and at least in the later scenes she gave the impression of being 'compassionate friend rather than tart scold' (*Shakespeare Survey 35*, p. 148). Irving Wardle, however, saw her as engaging in 'naggingly undiplomatic attacks on the tyrant Leontes' which she kept up 'right through to the statue scene' (review of the Barbican production, *The Times*, 29 July 1982); and Gareth Lloyd Evans considered that while she captured Paulina's 'audacity and forthrightness', she was a comic actress better suited to such parts as the Nurse in *Romeo and Juliet* and Mistress Quickly in *Henry IV* (*Stratford-upon-Avon Herald*, 10 July 1981). It is true that Sheila Hancock did play certain lines strongly for laughs. For example, in II iii when she brought the newborn child to Leontes she brushed aside the restraining courtiers with all the confidence of a wife accustomed to getting her own way, and she replied to the King's command to 'Force her hence' with a pugnacious 'Let him that makes but trifles of his eyes / First hand me' (62–3) which the audience hugely enjoyed. Similarly, to Leontes' refusal to accept the 'brat' as his she gave a retort which brought out the comic brusqueness of Shakespeare's lines to the full (95–7); and she got a well-deserved laugh when, with Leontes scowling his annoyance, she provocatively detailed the resemblance down to 'The pretty dimples of his chin and cheek; his smiles . . .' (101). However, the great virtue of her performance was that she was able, as Warren suggests, to modulate convincingly from honest, if somewhat burlesque, critic to equally honest adviser and even comforter. In both roles she projected Paulina as the consistent voice of true, natural feeling.

It is a testimony to the strength of Shakespeare's writing for the part of Paulina that it is a role which has attracted so many excellent performances from so many distinguished actresses. Perhaps more conventionally than Sheila Hancock, but with touches of humour that were still refreshingly brisk, both Brenda Bruce and Barbara Leigh-Hunt, in the 1969 and 1976 RSC productions respectively, gave interpretations which effectively countered the sick world of Leontes with healthy common sense (though Barbara Leigh-Hunt did so more gracefully, and Brenda Bruce, as the audience would have expected, in a more down-to-earth, no-nonsense vein). Subsequently, both gave the impression of sharpening the pangs of the King's remorse through the bluntness and acerbity of their comments – not, however, sadistically, but with the ultimately constructive purpose of bringing him to the level of self-realisation necessary before his final reunion with Hermione can come about.

In the 1980 television version another impressive performance came from Margaret Tyzack. The risk she ran was that her haughty, duchess-like manner (making her, at times, seem the bossy hospital matron) would dominate the screen and become positively overbearing. Her interruption of Leontes' restless torment in II iii to thrust the unwanted 'bastard' on him fully warranted his horrified 'Away with that audacious lady!' [42]; and when the courtiers tried to hush her she was loud and bold. But she was not merely shrewish. If Antigonus could not control her (giving some colour to Leontes' taunt at lines 74–5), her own *self*-control and innate authority made viewers feel the truth of her husband's defence of his handling of her:

> La you now, you hear.
> When she will take the rein, I let her run;
> But she'll not stumble.   [50–2]

The greatest virtue of Margaret Tyzack's performance lay in her ability to suggest, in spite of all, that the essential driving forces behind Paulina's behaviour were not wilfulness and waywardness, but compassion and humanity. The baby fired her indignation that anyone should be so perversely blind to it as Leontes; and his later penitence called forth an equally spontaneous response from her. Miss Tyzack's interpretation also made totally convincing the important executive role that Shakespeare assigns to Paulina (though it is shared with Camillo as well). She showed herself to be the strongest personality at the Sicilian Court, and to have a better head on her shoulders than any of the male courtiers.

14   THE COUNTRY CHARACTERS AND AUTOLYCUS

Mention has already been made of the differences between rustic and 'queenly' Perditas. In only one of the productions under discussion was there a corresponding Florizel – the RSC production of 1981, in which Philip Franks played the part. Franks did not, of course, speak with the accent of the stage rustic or behave in a yokel manner; it was rather his excessive naïveté which made him a counterpart of the simple-minded, easily duped country folk. The enthusiasm of this Florizel for Perdita seemed absurd rather than lyrically exuberant, though in all probability this was not the intention.

Regrettably, all four productions leaned towards banality in the characterisation of the Old Shepherd, the Clown and Mopsa and Dorcas. To some extent, it must be admitted, Shakespeare's writing provides an excuse for this. He shares with Thomas Hardy an affectionate, but slightly condescending, treatment of pure-bred country characters – a feature that seemed to be underlined by the otherwise bizarre Victorian dressing given to the characters of the sheep-shearing scene in Eyre's production.

The most original, and controversial, treatment of the sheep-shearing festival came from Trevor Nunn in 1969. Taking his cue from the reference to the twelve rustics 'that have made themselves all men of hair' [iv iv 323–4], he created a wild, whooping dance which led one critic to describe the scene as 'a rave-up interlude imported from "Hair" ' (*Morning Star*, 17 May 1969), and another to write disparagingly of 'a crew of hirsute hippies in beads and skins [made] to stand in for the life-affirming peasantry' (*The Times*, 16 May 1969). Bartholomeusz reports (p. 218) that Trevor Nunn did not, in fact, see the rock show *Hair* – which was a tremendous, and rather scandalous, success on the London stage in the late 1960s – till two or three months after his production of *The Winter's Tale* opened at Stratford. The truth probably is that both productions responded independently to the contemporary craze for 'pop' music and physically strenuous, indecorous dances, rather than that one was derived from the other. As with any such attempt to give a literary classic an intensely 'with-it' look, much of the reaction was hostile; and part of the intention was, no doubt, to shock. But the audience certainly found it a novel experience. As a style for the sheep-shearing festival it was a refreshing departure from the banality of the more usual mixture of folk song and morris dancing; and it was entirely successful in expressing that elemental vitality and primitive force which this part of the play must communicate if it is to come across effectively as a source of new life counteracting the poisoned atmosphere created in Acts I–III by Leontes' 'diseased opinion'. However, the dances were not all coarseness and crudeness; there was decorous lyricism as well, with the effect of contrast heightened by some reordering of the sequence of the text so that lines 322–39 (including the 'Saltiers'' dance) came in at line 183, only fifteen lines after the *dance of Shepherds and Shepherdesses*. At the very least, Nunn's innovation was a marvellous theatrical romp, which startled the audience into new attention to an over-familiar scene – with beneficial repercussions on its poetic as well as its prosaic elements.

In all productions of *The Winter's Tale* Autolycus, like Bottom in *A Midsummer Night's Dream*, comes near to stealing the show. Not only is this a brilliantly written part, but it offers (as no doubt it did in Jacobean times) ample scope for improvisation of comic business. Autolycus was 'littered under Mercury' and performs a very mercurial role. In the 1969 RSC production Derek Smith acted the part with burlesque energy, 'in the manner and gear of a discotheque comedian' (Ronald Boyden, *Observer*, 18 May 1969); and liberties were taken to modernise the text, to the extent that 'When daffodils begin to peer' [IV iii] lost its two final stanzas ('But shall I go mourn . . . And in the stocks avouch it'), while the remaining three were jazzed up and lengthened by the addition of pseudo-Shakespearean words of outright hedonism: 'Hey, hey, thrush and the jay, forget tomorrow and live today' (sung twice after the first stanza and once after the second), and 'Tumbling, tumbling in the hay, forget tomorrow and live today' (sung twice after the third stanza). In addition there was a liberal supply of comic business. The scene opened, for example, with Autolycus lying under a sheet. He woke, and stirred, and, as if still feeling the cold of winter, he shivered and rubbed himself. But, as he started to sing his song, he visibly warmed himself up, and the general temperature seemed to rise, till at the beginning of the third stanza ('The lark, that tirra-lyra chants') he felt the need to take off his coat and hat; and, after the completion of his song, to the delight of the audience he capered in a small circle.

The keynote for Autolycus is disguise, and in the 1976 RSC production this was emphasised in Michael Williams's almost furiously manic interpretation of the part by his seeming to be an 'Irish beggar at one moment, a rustic Santa Claus at another' (*Financial Times*, 7 June 1976). When he appeared in IV iv he was supposedly transformed by his white beard and large spectacles, and the red and green coat he wore was opened to give the gawping rustics tantalising glimpses of his pedlar's tawdry stock-in-trade. Later in the scene, the exchange of clothes with Florizel was played with uproarious farce as the other characters on stage virtually pulled his trousers off him. All this made it hard for the audience to keep their minds on what was being said; but it was generally in keeping with the visually striking, gaudily costumed, and naïvely zestful primitiveness of the Barton–Nunn version of the sheep-shearing festival.

It was, however, in the 1981 RSC production, in which Geoffrey Hutchings played Autolycus, that the disguise element was really given its head. Already a courtier disguised as a beaten and robbed traveller, this Autolycus made himself into a comically implausible scarecrow to 'hide' from the outraged crowd who wanted to lynch him for his thieving; and at the sheep-shearing he seemed to be all things to all men, doing conjuring tricks in a costume resembling that of a down-at-heel Victorian impresario, singing popular songs like the standard music-hall comedian, and delivering his professional patter with what sometimes sounded like a cockney accent and sometimes did not. And, to cap it all, the exchange of costumes with Florizel was so complete that even the moustache was included. The comedian seemed to be running riot – 'doing his own thing', and, in true Autolycus style, always getting away with it. Yet this multiplicity of disguises and series of farcical impromptus none the less served the play's ultimate purpose by emphasising the very changeableness of illusion.

In the BBC television production of 1980 the unusual, but highly successful, choice of an already well-known comic personality, Rikki Fulton (adept in mocking Glaswegian speed cops and Calvinist ministers saying their pieces on the media's 'God spots'), yielded a very 'knowing' Autolycus. He shamelessly played to the camera, and insinuated himself with the viewer as expertly as with a live audience. At his first entrance in IV iii, corresponding with the transformation of the set into one glowing with golden-yellow light (*see above*, p. 56), he carried a heavy pack on his back, which he unfolded to reveal his 'traffic' of stolen sheets. After removing this he sat down and chatted confidentially to the viewer while paring an apple. As the Clown entered he gleefully exclaimed, 'A prize! A prize!', shifted his pack out of sight, and hid behind the tree. The Clown's naïve preoccupation with his list of purchases for the feast gave Autolycus plenty of time to creep out and inspect his back for signs of anything that might be worth stealing. Having decided that this was a potentially profitable victim, Autolycus then took off his coat, moved to up-stage left, and threw himself down on the ground, making sure that he attracted the Clown's attention by groaning out, 'O that ever I was born!' [49]. When the Clown touched him he affected to feel great pain – 'O good sir, softly, good sir! I fear, sir, my shoulder-blade is out' [71–2]. This made the Clown so concerned that he put his hands under Autolycus's arms to lift him up as gently as possible, thus giving the thief the perfect opportunity for stealing the purse which he had already reconnoitred. (And, of course, Rikki Fulton made the most of the irony in 'You ha' done me a charitable office' [75].) When offered money he naturally affected to be hurt by the very thought of it, taking care, however, to restrain the Clown's hand from reaching for the now missing purse; and more 'knowing' irony was shared with the viewer when he sketched his own character – 'I know this man well . . .' [91–7] – and, pointing to his ragged clothes, added, 'that's the rogue that put me into this apparel' [100–1]. More business was used to prolong the purse joke when he replied to the Clown's compassionate 'How do you now?' with, 'Sweet sir, much better than I was . . .' [108], patting the place where he had tucked away the stolen item as he did so; and, finally, after the Clown's exit, he chuckled to himself as he murmured, 'Your purse is not hot enough to purchase your spice' [116].

In this production, as in earlier ones, the enthusiastic build-up provided by the Servant's words at iv iv 183–212 made Autolycus's second entrance almost as good as his first. When he appeared he was disguised yet again by beard and moustache, and the Clown carried his pack for him, already opened to reveal a shelf displaying his colourful knick-knacks. He was a great crowd-puller – though, notwithstanding Shakespeare's implicit stage direction, '. . . let him approach singing' [213], more by virtue of his ability to spin a yarn than his tunefulness. It was his sensational description of what his ballads contained that fascinated his rustic audience, and his adroitness in guessing what would most appeal to them (hence his dropping in the sexually titillating information that one of his ballads was sung by a woman 'turned into a cold fish for she would not exchange flesh with one that loved her' [277–8]).

At his third entrance [592] Autolycus came in with his 'disguise' beard dangling in his hand and laughing over the folly of Honesty; and the word 'all' in 'I have sold all my trumpery' [594] was exaggeratedly prolonged as he mockingly turned his eyes up to heaven. He quickly donned his hat and beard again as Camillo came over to him, and this prepared him for yet another change, at the end of which he was left in Florizel's superior rural disguise. With a typical Rikki Fulton touch, he peered over Camillo's shoulder at lines 658–63, as if to say, 'What's this – it sounds a rum business to me' – thus getting round the slight awkwardness always created by Camillo's 'betrayal' of Florizel and Perdita, as well as heightening the general sense at this point in the play that potentially tragic action is turning into comic intrigue. Similarly, in the dialogue which followed between him and the Old Shepherd and the Clown, his deliberately overdone superiority of manner as he played the greater courtier to their rustic credulity effectively turned terror into burlesque. In every one of his many forms of disguise he also managed to combine relish for his roles with an eye to the financial main chance (his neat use of the finger-rubbing gesture for money was enough to convey the idea of a bribe as he said, 'Being something gently considered, I'll bring you . . .' [790–1]); and his final speech, 'If I had a mind to be honest, I see Fortune would not suffer me . . .' [825ff.] rounded off the whole series of his disguise permutations with a fittingly amoral, but altogether comic, complacency.

15 'EXIT PURSUED BY A BEAR'

In all productions of *The Winter's Tale* there are certain scenes and incidents that create special problems for the director. The best known, or most notorious, of these is the stage direction in III iii, '*Exit, pursued by a bear.*' The sight of a bear (known, of course, to be an 'extra' in a bearskin) lolloping over the stage in pursuit of Antigonus will always strike some members of the audience as comic; and, though I have argued in Part One of this book that such laughter is not inimical to the desired dramatic effect of transition from tragedy to comedy, most modern directors have not cared to risk an effect of outright farce. Consequently they have tended towards symbolic rather than realistic bears.

In his 1969 RSC production Trevor Nunn opted for a huge and terrifying animal of which David Perry (head of the RSC wardrobe department) is reported as saying, 'It is made of goatskin with expanded polythene on a bamboo frame. It is a splendid specimen. The actor will have to wear special eight-inch high boots to lumber across the stage' (*Birmingham Post*, 16 May 1969). Its effect in performance, aided once more by stroboscopic lighting, was to give Antigonus's death a weirdly terrifying and yet unearthly dimension. Hardened theatre critics, however, were prone to engage in sardonic banter at its expense. Thus Hilary Spurling wittily described the bear as 'rearing up some twelve feet tall as his victim bolts across the floor, so that Antigonus becomes a squirming dwarf, grappled and finally enveloped, the pair of them dwarfed in turn by the set's walls rearing at least forty feet above'. In Spurling's view the episode spelt, not catastrophe, but a kind of burlesque: 'the whole calamity has a nice turn of speed, and an even nicer blend of visual elegance and nonchalant absurdity' (*Spectator*, 23 May 1969).

The 1976 RSC production was the one which seemed most bear-conscious. As already indicated, bear motifs figured largely in the decor, and playful bear hunts in the early scenes anticipated the climactic moment of III iii. Yet the actual presentation of Antigonus's death was curiously anti-climactic. In an attempt to give the bear a mythological rather than realistic dimension, it was stylistically represented by an actor carrying skulls and wearing a mask which was subsequently removed to reveal the Chorus who speaks to the audience as Time. (The justification for this was somewhat desperately provided in the programme by a page of quotations under the punning title, 'The Bear Facts'.) Finally, the 'exit' itself became a procession rather than a 'pursuit', in which Antigonus was seemingly 'ushered' or 'escorted', as reviewers variously expressed it, off stage by the bear (cf. *New Statesman*, 11 June 1976, and *Observer*, 13 June 1976).

In the 1980 television version Jane Howell settled for the relatively simple device of showing a bear's head in close-up, and she chose to omit the actual chase; but, on the stage once more (at Stratford-upon-Avon, in his 1981 RSC production) Ronald Eyre opted for the huge image of a bear, glimpsed in a flash of lightning, and by so doing seemed to suggest that this was Nature's preternaturally sanctioned revenge on Antigonus for allowing himself to become the agent, albeit a reluctant one, of the innocent baby's exposure and death (or what Leontes intended to be its death and Antigonus accepts as such).

Of these devices perhaps Nunn's and Eyre's were the most successful, creating as they did a nightmarish, sensational impression which combined terror with the non-realistic dimension appropriate to 'an old tale'. They showed that the notorious problem is capable of solution, and that perhaps the boldest method is the best.

16 CONCLUSION

A play in performance inevitably falls short of an imaginary, ideal performance, but even a flawed performance in the live theatre is an essential experience complementary to the study of the text in the classroom or in the leisure and privacy of one's home. It was the context of the theatre (though, admittedly, a very different one in many respects from that of the present day) which Shakespeare had in mind when writing all his plays; and the sense of theatricality – of scenes and language

which imply the presence of an audience, and that audience's
reciprocal awareness of the fact of stage performance – is highly
characteristic of all of them, and not least of *The Winter's Tale*.
The element of the marvellous which it derives from the
romance tradition might seem to be incompatible with dramatic presentation; the particular source of *The Winter's Tale*,
Greene's *Pandosto*, is a narrative, not a play, and it is possible in
such a form to gloss over incidents which might strike one as too
absurd for direct representation in front of an audience. But
this seems not to have worried Shakespeare. He frequently
alludes to the very preposterousness of what is happening, but
instead of nervously apologising for the inadequacies of the
dramatic medium he seems to revel in the challenge which it
offers. In v ii he ingeniously contrives a narrative situation
within a dramatic context, as the story of Perdita is told at
second hand, rather than directly enacted: and it is into this
scene that he especially concentrates romantic absurdities that
are 'Like an old tale still, which will have matter to rehearse,
though credit be asleep'. The audience is thus invited to laugh
at an old-fashioned tall story, while at the same time enjoying a
piece of dramatised narration which is deeply moving. In the
following scene they also see a statue come to life in a way that
ought, by ordinary standards of plausibility, to be a gross
exhibition of the inadequacy of drama to handle the more
extravagant features of romance. For Shakespeare, however,
this becomes the opportunity for a theatrical *tour de force* which,
as the history of the play in performance testifies, always comes
off brilliantly. The characters on stage are ostensibly given a
choice: either to 'awake their faith', or, for those who think it is
'unlawful business', to depart. The choice is unreal, of course,
for these characters are only puppets, doing and saying what
has been set down for them. But the theatre audience *can* do
either; and in effect do both – that is to say, they believe and
disbelieve simultaneously, yielding themselves to the theatrical
experience which weaves its magic spell around them, and yet
retaining a sense that what they witness is 'romance', with all
which that implies of both scepticism and illuminating delight.

Above all, the audience gathered in the theatre become a
collective entity, without (and in this respect they are quite
unlike a crowd at a football match or a political meeting)

surrendering their private sensibilities and thoughts. They engage in a relationship with the actors on stage, and through them with the total action that constitutes the dramatic form. Isolated from each other their response would not be the same. This, indeed, is one of the problems of presenting Shakespeare on television. As we have seen, Jane Howell's BBC television production of *The Winter's Tale* tries in various ways to overcome this; but it is most successful where it is able to tap the skills of an exceptionally talented comedian, Rikki Fulton, who has learnt to treat the camera as an audience. Thanks to him the Autolycus scenes become an audience–actor conspiracy, notwithstanding the absence of a physically present audience to share in the comic business. But, as Stanley Wells remarks in his review of this production, the 'medium' has a tendency to 'reduce the message'. The absence of collective response, combined with the smallness of the image and the limited amount of action it can encompass, 'all too easily circumscribes, concentrating attention, reducing perspective, diminishing stature' (*TLS*, 20 Feb 1981). This was particularly noticeable in iii ii of the television version, where a sense of public ceremony before a large gathering of spectators was essential to the proper effect of Hermione's trial – 'here standing / To prate and talk for life and honour 'fore / Who please to come and hear' [39–41]. Jane Howell sought to overcome the limitations of the television screen, and the isolation of audience from performers, by having the camera peer down on the scene as from a tree into which onlookers have climbed. The viewer was thus invited to identify himself with the spectators. It is doubtful, however, if this was the effect for many viewers; and in any case the subsequent dependence on close-ups – a technical necessity for television drama – caused the abandonment of any such sense of public participation. The close-up, so convenient for soliloquy, turned the trial into a private affair totally lacking in the reverberation created in the theatre when the principals interact with the stage spectators and both with the collective-*cum*-individual presence of the audience.

Not that this effect is automatically achieved in the theatre. There was a point of similarity between the television production and Ronald Eyre's 1981 RSC production in that Eyre likewise sought to involve the audience by treating them as the spectators of the trial scene. The triple relationship was thus reduced to a dual one, and the audience was pressured into surrendering its privilege of simultaneous sympathy and detachment. This unhappy result was also compounded by the forbidding emptiness of the stage – part of a strategy to emphasise the artifice of the play as a whole. Eyre's dummies (*see above*, p. 52) too forcibly reminded the audience of the arbitrariness of the performance. It was a Brechtian 'alienation' device inappropriate to the far subtler balancing of scepticism and 'faith' which Shakespeare's text implies.

There was, however, this much to be said for Ronald Eyre's production: its willingness to rely on the imagination of the audience rather than supply images too lavishly, and its insistence that art should be acknowledged as art and performance as performance, threw the onus of illusion back where it should be thrown, on the actors and the words. Indeed, the 1981 RSC production may be regarded as something of a reaction against the powerfully assertive productions of its RSC predecessors in 1969 and 1976. The latter were very much director's theatre, in which interpretation – a particular view of the text – dominated, and devices, often of a very original and exciting kind, were liberally employed to bounce the audience into accepting a modern meaning, and to experience the play as a tract for the times. Hence the tremendous effect of Trevor Nunn's use at Stratford in 1969 of stroboscopic lighting and 'freezing' and the sheer panache of his pop-music sheep-shearing festival – which, the more it scandalised its audiences, the more it delighted them with its almost brash determination to show Shakespeare as our contemporary. Of the four productions discussed in this book, although it was the earliest, it was strictly the most memorable. For better, for worse, it stamped on the minds of a whole generation of theatre-goers a very bold caricature (if it is possible to use that word without too derogatory an implication) of *The Winter's Tale* which stirred them to a realisation of the play's quite unacademic immediacy. At the same time it almost blocked out other images. In a remarkable effort of self-criticism Nunn joined with John Barton in the RSC production of 1976 to present a fairy-story version which would be strongly enough coloured to stand out even against the bright glare of his own '69 production. The result, however, was even bolder caricature and a kind of desperate underlining of the solstitial extremities now imposed on the play by its 'Scandinavian' motifs. This, too, was a very considerable theatrical success, and paradoxically achieved contemporaneity through its modernist accent on primitiveness and non-representational design. Yet it was equally director's theatre.

It would be churlish to ignore the contribution which these two productions have made to our present-day understanding and appreciation of *The Winter's Tale*. They have, it is fair to say, done even more than the Shakespeare scholars and critics to reinstate this play as a recognised masterpiece of drama. By making it come alive in the theatre they have demonstrated what most of all needed to be demonstrated – its essential stageworthiness; while also demanding that it be taken seriously. Their danger, however, is that they encourage directorial addiction. After them it is difficult not to crave vivid, exciting, 'with-it' performances. Their influence was seen even in the 'Brechtian' 1981 RSC production of Ronald Eyre: if his dummies symbolised reaction against the RSC tradition, the pageant of Time and the Victorian hotch-potch of his sheepshearing festival still bore witness to the feeling generated by Nunn and Barton that strong images are the way to make the play live. By comparison Jane Howell's BBC version not only suffered the disadvantages which in television Shakespeare are inevitable, but also seemed uninventive and visually tame. This was not, of course, essentially true. There was inventiveness enough in Jane Howell's production, but it did not brilliantly project a distinct interpretation like Nunn's and Barton's. The text was left rather more to speak for itself.

My conclusion is not that the time is ripe for more of Jane Howell and less of Trevor Nunn, but rather that text and performance be kept in proper balance. Directorial theatre is the most stimulating thing we have known in recent productions of *The Winter's Tale*, and there is room, no doubt, for more innovations of the sort that only great directors can provide. But it is to be hoped that the future will also bring more even-toned performances which leave us to do more of the work of interpretation for ourselves. There is always more to be found in the text than in any given performance, no matter how brilliant. Equally, however, what we find in the text ought always to be conditioned by a sense of how it might be realised in performance; and this most crucial sense of theatrical viability is something to which both ambitious directorial productions and those of a more self-effacing kind alike contribute.

READING LIST

The edition used throughout is that by Ernest Schanzer, New Penguin Shakespeare (1969). The Arden edition, ed. J. H. P. Pafford (1963) is equally recommended. Useful material is also to be found in H. H. Furness's Variorum edition (Philadelphia, 1898) and in the BBC Television Shakespeare edition (1981). For the most detailed treatment of sources and reprinting of texts see *Narrative and Dramatic Sources of Shakespeare*, ed. Geoffrey Bullough, vol. VIII (1975). Schanzer comments on Shakespeare's debt to *Pandosto* and the Greek romance tradition; and further material on Greek romance will be found in S. L. Wolff, *The Greek Romances in Elizabethan Prose Fiction* (New York, 1912), and Carol Gesner, *Shakespeare and the Greek Romance* (University of Kentucky, 1970).

The most thoroughgoing critical study of the play is Fitzroy Pyle, *'The Winter's Tale': A Commentary on the Structure* (1969). Also recommended are S. L. Bethel, *'The Winter's Tale': A Study* (1947); A. D. Nuttall, *Shakespeare: 'The Winter's Tale'* (1966); G. Wilson Knight, *The Crown of Life* (1947); Derek Traversi, *Shakespeare: The Last Phase* (1954); and the Casebook edited by Kenneth Muir (1968).

With regard to performance, Pafford includes a brief stage history in the Arden edition (Appendix III); but the fullest account is to be found in Dennis Bartholomeusz, *'The Winter's Tale' in Performance in England and America, 1611–1976* (Cambridge, 1982). Mention should also be made of two MA theses lodged at the University of Warwick: Christine Wallwork, *'The Winter's Tale* in Production' (1976), which gives an account of the 1976 production; and Kathleen Gledhill, 'Emblematic Figures in *The Winter's Tale*' (1981), which includes comment on aspects of the 1969, 1976 and 1981 productions. See also the following: Alan Brissenden, *Shakespeare and the Dance* (1981); John Russell Brown, 'Laughter in the Last Plays', *Stratford-upon-Avon Studies 8* (1966); Nevill Coghill, 'Six Points of Stage-Craft in *The Winter's Tale*', *Shakespeare Survey 11* (1958) and its sequel, William H. Matchett, 'Some Dramatic Techniques in *The Winter's Tale*', *Shakespeare Survey 22* (1969); Inga-Stina Ewbank, 'The Triumph of Time in *The Winter's Tale*', *Review of English Literature*, vol. v (1964).

INDEX OF NAMES